William Craft (1824–1900) and **Ellen Craft** (1826–1891) were slaves from Macon, Georgia in the United States who escaped to the North in December 1848. Their daring escape was widely publicized, making them among the most

CONTENTS

RUNNING A THOUSAND MILES FOR FREEDOM

THE DARING ESCAPE OF WILLIAM AND ELLEN CRAFT

WILLIAM AND ELLEN CRAFT

Paperback: 978-811900792-9

Printed by:

Sanage Publishing House LLP
Mumbai, India

sanagepublishing@gmail.com

PREFACE

Having heard while in Slavery that "God made of one blood all nations of men," and also that the American Declaration of Independence says, that "We hold these truths to be self-evident, that all men are created equal; that they are endowed by their Creator with certain inalienable rights; that among these, are life, liberty, and the pursuit of happiness;" we could not understand by what right we were held as "chattels." Therefore, we felt perfectly justified in undertaking the dangerous and exciting task of "running a thousand miles" in order to obtain those rights which are so vividly set forth in the Declaration.

I beg those who would know the particulars of our journey, to peruse these pages.

This book is not intended as a full history of the life of my wife, nor of myself; but merely as an account of our escape; together with other matter which I hope may be the means of creating in some minds a deeper abhorrence of the sinful and abominable practice of enslaving and brutifying our fellow-creatures.

Without stopping to write a long apology for offering this little volume to the public, I shall commence at once to pursue my simple story.

W. CRAFT.

12, CAMBRIDGE ROAD, HAMMERSMITH,

LONDON.

PART I.

"God gave us only over beast, fish, fowl,

Dominion absolute: that right we hold
By his donation. But man over man
He made not lord; such title to himself
Reserving, human left from human free."

MILTON.

My wife and myself were born in different towns in the State of Georgia, which is one of the principal slave States. It is true, our condition as slaves was not by any means the worst but the mere idea that we were held as chattels, and deprived of all legal right the thought that we had to give up our hard earnings to a tyrant, to enable him to live in idleness and luxury, the thought that we could not call the bones and sinews that God gave us our own: but above all, the fact that another man had the power to tear from our cradle the new-born babe and sell it in the shambles like a brute, and then scourge us if we dared to lift a finger to save it from such a fate, haunted us for years.

But in December 1848, a plan suggested itself that proved quite successful and in eight days after it was first thought of, we were free from the horrible trammels of slavery, rejoicing and praising God in the glorious sunshine of liberty.

My wife's first master was her father and her mother his slave, and the latter is still the slave of his widow.

Notwithstanding my wife being of African ex- traction on her mother's side, she is almost white in fact, she is so nearly so that the tyrannical old lady to whom she first belonged became so annoyed, at finding her frequently mistaken for a child of the family, that she gave her when eleven years of age to a daughter, as a wedding present. This separated my wife from her mother, and also from several other dear friends. But the incessant cruelty of her old mistress made the change of owners or treatment so desirable, that she did not grumble much at this cruel separation.

It may be remembered that slavery in America is not at all confined to persons of any particular complexion; there are a very large number of slaves as white as any one; but as the evidence of a slave is not admitted in court against a free white person, it is almost impossible for a white child, after having been kidnapped and sold into or reduced to slavery, in a part of the country where it is not known (as often is the case), ever to recover its freedom.

I have myself conversed with several slaves who told me that their parents were white and free but that they were stolen away from them and sold when quite young. As they could not tell their address, and also as the parents did not know what had become of their lost and dear little ones, of course all traces of each other were gone.

The following facts are sufficient to prove, that he who has the power, and is inhuman enough to trample upon the sacred rights of the weak, cares nothing for race or colour:

In March 1818, three ships arrived at New Orleans, bringing several hundred German emigrants from the province of Alsace, on the lower Rhine. Among them were Daniel Muller and his two daughters, Dorothea and Salome, whose mother had died on the passage. Soon after his arrival, Muller, taking with him his two daughters, both young children, went up the river to Attakapas parish, to work on the plantation of John F. Miller. A few weeks later, his relatives, who had remained at New Orleans, learned that he had died of the fever of the country. They immediately sent for the two girls, but they had disappeared and the relatives, notwithstanding repeated and persevering inquiries and researches, could find no traces of them. They were at length given up for dead. Dorothea was never again heard of, nor was anything known of Salome from 1818 till 1843.

In the summer of that year, Madame Karl, a German woman who had come over in the same ship with the Mullers, was passing through a street in New Orleans, and accidentally saw Salome in a wine-shop, belonging to Louis Belmonte, by whom she was held as a slave. Madame Karl recognized her at once and carried her to the house of another German woman, Mrs. Schubert, who was Salome's cousin and godmother, and who no sooner set eyes on her than, without having any intimation that the discovery had been previously made, she unhesitatingly exclaimed, "My God! here is the long-lost Salome Muller."

The Law Reporter, in its account of this case, says:

"As many of the German emigrants of 1818 as could be gathered together were brought to the house of Mrs. Schubert, and every one of the numbers who had any recollection of the little girl upon the passage, or any acquaintance with her father and mother, immediately identified the woman before them as the long-lost Salome Muller. By all these witnesses, who appeared at the trial, the identity was fully established. The family resemblance in every feature was declared to be so remarkable, that some of the witnesses did not hesitate to say that they should know her among ten thousand; that they were as certain the plaintiff was Salome Muller, the daughter of Daniel and Dorothea Muller, as of their own existence."

Among the witnesses who appeared in Court was the midwife who had assisted at the birth of Salome. She testified to the existence of certain peculiar marks upon the body of the child, which were found, exactly as described, by the surgeons who were appointed by the Court to make an examination for the purpose.

There was no trace of African descent in any feature of Salome Muller. She had long, straight, black hair, hazel eyes, thin lips, and a Roman nose. The complexion of her face and neck was as dark as that of the darkest brunette. It appears, however, that, during the twenty-five years of her servitude, she had been exposed to the sun's rays in the hot climate of Louisiana, with head and neck unsheltered, as is customary with the female slaves, while labouring in the cotton or the sugar field. Those parts of her person which had been shielded from the sun were comparatively white.

Belmonte, the pretended owner of the girl, had obtained possession of her by an act of sale from John F. Miller, the planter in whose service Salome's father died. This Miller was a man of consideration and substance, owning large sugar estates, and bearing a high reputation for honour and honesty and for indulgent treatment of his slaves. It was testified on the trial that he had said to Belmonte, a few weeks after the sale of Salome, "that she was white, and had as much right to her freedom as anyone and was only to be retained in slavery by care and kind treatment." The broker who negotiated the sale from Miller to Belmonte, in 1838, testified in Court that he then thought, and still thought, that the girl was white!

The case was elaborately argued on both sides but was at length decided in favour of the girl, by the Supreme Court declaring that "she was free and white, and therefore unlawfully held in bondage."

The Rev. George Bourne, of Virginia, in his Picture of Slavery, published in 1834, relates the case of a white boy who, at the age of seven, was stolen from his home in Ohio, tanned and stained in such a way that he could not be distinguished from a person of colour, and then sold as a slave in Virginia. At the age of twenty, he made his escape, by running away, and happily succeeded in rejoining his parents.

I have known worthless white people to sell their own free children into slavery; and, as there are good-for-nothing white as well as coloured persons everywhere, no one, perhaps, will wonder at such inhuman transactions particularly in the Southern States of America, where I believe there is a greater want of humanity and high principle amongst the whites, than among any other civilized people in the world.

I know that those who are not familiar with the work of "the peculiar institution," can scarcely imagine anyone so totally devoid of all-natural affection as to sell his own offspring into return-less bondage. But Shakespeare, that great observer of human nature, says:

"With caution judge of probabilities.
Things deemed unlikely, e'en impossible,
Experience often shews us to be true."

My wife's new mistress was decidedly more humane than the majority of her class. My wife has always given her credit for not exposing her to many of the worst features of slavery. For instance, it is a common practice in the slave States for ladies, when angry with their maids, to send them to the calybuce sugar-house, or to some other place established for the purpose of punishing slaves, and have them severely flogged and I am sorry it is a fact, that the villains to whom those defenceless creatures are sent, not only flog them as they are ordered, but frequently compel them to submit to the greatest indignity. Oh! if there is any one thing under the wide canopy of heaven, horrible enough to stir a man's soul, and to make his very blood boil, it is the thought of his dear wife, his unprotected sister, or his young and virtuous daughters, struggling to save themselves from falling a prey to such demons!

It always appears strange to me that anyone who was not born a slaveholder and steeped to the very core in the demoralizing atmosphere of the Southern States, can in any way palliate slavery. It is still more surprising to see virtuous ladies looking with patience upon, and remaining indifferent to, the existence of a system that exposes nearly two millions of their own sex in the manner I have mentioned and that too in a professedly free and Christian country. There is, however, great consolation in knowing that God is just, and will not let the oppressor of the weak, and the spoiler of the virtuous, escape unpunished here and hereafter.

I believe a similar retribution to that which destroyed Sodom is hanging over the slaveholders. My sincere prayer is that they may not provoke God, by persisting in a reckless course of wickedness, to pour out his consuming wrath upon them.

I must now return to our history.

My old master had the reputation of being a very humane and Christian man, but he thought nothing of selling my poor old father, and dear aged mother, at separate times, to different persons, to be dragged off never to behold each other again, till summoned to appear before the great tribunal of heaven. But, oh! what a happy meeting it will be on that day for those faithful souls. I say a happy meeting, because I never saw persons more devoted to the service of God than they. But how will the case stand with those reckless traffickers in human flesh and blood, who plunged the poisonous dagger of separation into those loving hearts which God had for so many years closely joined together nay, sealed as it were with his own hands for the eternal courts of heaven? It is not for me to say what will become of those heartless tyrants. I must leave them in the hands of an all-wise and just God, who will, in his own good time, and in his own way, avenge the wrongs of his oppressed people.

My old master also sold a dear brother and a sister, in the same manner as he did my father and mother. The reason he assigned for disposing of my parents, as well as of several other aged slaves, was, that "they were getting old, and would soon become valueless in the market, and therefore he intended to sell off all the old stock and buy in a young lot." A most disgraceful conclusion for a man to come to, who made such great professions of religion!

This shameful conduct gave me a thorough hatred, not for true Christianity, but for slave- holding piety.

My old master, then, wishing to make the most of the rest of his slaves, apprenticed a brother and myself out to learn trades: he to a blacksmith and myself to a cabinetmaker. If a slave has a good trade, he will let or sell for more than a person without one, and many slave- holders have their slaves taught trades on this account. But before our time expired, my old master wanted money, so he sold my brother, and then mortgaged my sister, a dear girl about four-teen years of age, and myself, then about sixteen, to one of the banks, to get money to speculate in cotton. This we knew nothing of at the moment; but time rolled on, the money became due, my master was unable to meet his payments, so the bank had us placed upon the auction stand and sold to the highest bidder.

My poor sister was sold first: she was knocked down to a planter who resided at some distance in the country. Then I was called upon to the stand. While the auctioneer was crying the bids, I saw the man that had purchased my sister getting her into a cart, to take her to his home. I at once asked a slave friend who was standing near the platform, to run and ask the gentleman if he would please to wait till I was sold, in order that I might have an opportunity of bidding her goodbye. He sent me word back that he had some distance to go and could not wait.

I then turned to the auctioneer, fell upon my knees, and humbly prayed to him to let me just step down and bid my last sister farewell. But, instead of granting me this request, he grasped me by the neck, and in a commanding tone of voice and with a violent oath, exclaimed, "Get up! You can do the wench no good; therefore, there is no use in your seeing her."

On rising, I saw the cart in which she sat moving slowly off; and, as she clasped her hands with a grasp that indicated despair, and looked pitifully round towards me, I also saw the large silent tears trickling down her cheeks. She made a farewell bow and buried her face in her lap. This seemed more than I could bear. It appeared to swell my aching heart to its utmost. But before I could fairly recover, the poor girl was gone; gone, and I have never had the good for- tune to see her from that day to this! Perhaps I should have never heard of her again, had it not been for the untiring efforts of my good old mother, who became free a few years ago by purchase, and, after a great deal of difficulty, found my sister residing with a family in Mississippi. My mother at once wrote to me, informing me of the fact, and requesting me to do something to get her free; and I am happy to say that, partly by lecturing occasionally, and through the sale of an engraving of my wife in the disguise in which she escaped, together with the extreme kind- ness and generosity of Miss Burdett Coutts, Mr. George Richardson of Plymouth, and a few other friends, I have nearly accomplished this. It would be to me a great and ever-glorious achievement to restore my sister to our dear mother, from whom she was forcibly driven in early life.

I was knocked down to the cashier of the bank to which we were mortgaged and ordered to return to the cabinet shop where I previously worked.

But the thought of the harsh auctioneer not allowing me to bid my dear sister farewell, sent red-hot indignation darting like lightning through every vein. It quenched my tears, and appeared to set my brain on fire, and made me crave for power to avenge our wrongs! But alas! we were only slaves, and had no legal rights; consequently, we were compelled to smother our wounded feelings, and crouch beneath the iron heel of despotism.

I must now give an account of our escape but, before doing so, it may be well to quote a few passages from the fundamental laws of slavery; in order to give some idea of the legal as well as the social tyranny from which we fled.

According to the law of Louisiana, "A slave is one who is in the power of a master to whom he belongs. The master may sell him, dispose of his person, his industry and his labour; he can do nothing, possess nothing, nor acquire anything but what must belong to his master." Civil Code, art. 35.

In South Carolina it is expressed in the following language: "Slaves shall be deemed, sold, taken, reputed and judged in law to be chattels personal in the hands of their owners and possessors, and their executors, administrators, and assigns, to all intents, constructions, and purposes whatsoever. 2 Brevard's Digest, 229.

The Constitution of Georgia has the following (Art. 4, sec. 12): "Any person who shall maliciously dismember or deprive a slave of life, shall suffer such punishment as would be inflicted in case the like offence had been committed on a free white person, and on the like proof, except in case of insurrection of such slave, and unless SUCH DEATH SHOULD HAPPEN BY ACCIDENT IN GIVING SUCH SLAVE MODERATE CORRECTION."—Prince's Digest, 559.

I have known slaves to be beaten to death, but as they died under "moderate correction," it was quite lawful and of course the murderers were not interfered with.

"If any slave, who shall be out of the house or plantation where such slave shall live, or shall be usually employed, or without some white person in company with such slave, shall refuse to submit to undergo the examination of any white person, (let him be ever so drunk or crazy), it shall be lawful for such white person to pursue, apprehend, and moderately correct such slave; and if such slave shall assault and strike such white person, such slave may be LAWFULLY KILLED."—2 Brevard's Digest, 231.

"Provided always," says the law, "that such striking be not done by the command and in the defence of the person or property of the owner, or other person having the government of such slave; in which case the slave shall be wholly excused."

According to this law, if a slave, by the direction of his overseer, strike a white person who is beating said overseer's pig, "the slave shall be wholly excused." But should the bondman, of his own accord, fight to defend his wife or should his terrified daughter instinctively raise her hand and strike the wretch who attempts to violate her chastity, he or she shall, saith the model republican law, suffer death.

From having been myself a slave for nearly twenty-three years, I am quite prepared to say that the practical working of slavery is worse than the odious laws by which it is governed.

At an early age we were taken by the persons who held us as property to Macon, the largest town in the interior of the State of Georgia, at which place we became acquainted with each other for several years before our marriage; in fact, our marriage was postponed for some time simply because one of the unjust and worse than Pagan laws under which we lived compelled all children of slave mothers to follow their condition. That is to say, the father of the slave may be the President of the Republic; but if the mother should be a slave at the infant's birth, the poor child is ever legally doomed to the same cruel fate.

It is a common practice for gentlemen (if I may call them such), moving in the highest circles of society, to be the fathers of children by their slaves, whom they can and do sell with the greatest impunity and the more pious, beautiful, and virtuous the girls are, the greater the price they bring, and that too for the most infamous purposes.

Any man with money (let him be ever such a rough brute), can buy a beautiful and virtuous girl, and force her to live with him in a criminal connection and as the law says a slave shall have no higher appeal than the mere will of the master, she cannot escape, unless it be by flight or death.

In endeavouring to reconcile a girl to her fate, the master sometimes says that he would marry her if it was not unlawful. * However, he will always consider her to be his wife, and will treat her as such; and she, on the other hand, may regard him as her lawful husband; and if they have any children, they will be free and well educated.

I am in duty bound to add, that while a great majority of such men care nothing for the happiness of the women with whom they live, nor for the children of whom they are the fathers, there are those to be found, even in that heterogeneous mass of licentious monsters, who are true to their pledges. But as the woman and her children are legally the property of the man, who stands in the anomalous relation to them of husband and father, as well as master, they are liable to be seized and sold for his debts, should he become involved.

There are several cases on record where such persons have been sold and separated for life. I know of some myself, but I have only space to glance at one.

I knew a very humane and wealthy gentleman, that bought a woman, with whom he lived as his

*** It is unlawful in the slave States for any one of purely European descent to intermarry with a person of African extraction; though a white man may live with as many coloured women as he pleases without materially damaging his reputation in Southern society wife. They brought up a family of children, among whom were three nearly white, well educated, and beautiful girls.**

On the father being suddenly killed it was found that he had not left a will but as the family had always heard him say that he had no surviving relatives, they felt that their liberty and property were quite secured to them, and, knowing the insults to which they were exposed, now their protector was no more, they were making preparations to leave for a free State.

But, poor creatures, they were soon sadly undeceived. A villain residing at a distance, hearing of the circumstance, came forward and swore that he was a relative of the deceased and as this man bore, or assumed, Mr. Slator's name, the case was brought before one of those horrible tribunals, presided over by a second Judge Jeffreys, and calling itself a court of justice, but before whom no coloured person, nor an abolitionist, was ever known to get his full rights.

A verdict was given in favour of the plaintiff, whom the better portion of the community thought had willfully conspired to cheat the family.

The heartless wretch not only took the ordinary property, but actually had the aged and friendless widow, and all her fatherless children, except Frank, a fine young man about twenty-two years of age, and Mary, a very nice girl, a little younger than her brother, brought to the auction stand and sold to the highest bidder. Mrs. Slator had cash enough, that her husband and master left, to purchase the liberty of herself and children; but on her attempting to do so, the pusillanimous scoundrel, who had robbed them of their freedom, claimed the money as his property and poor creature, she had to give it up. According to law, as will be seen hereafter, a slave cannot own anything. The old lady never recovered from her sad affliction.

At the sale she was brought up first, and after being vulgarly criticized, in the presence of all her distressed family, was sold to a cotton planter, who said he wanted the "proud old critter to go to his plantation, to look after the little woolly heads, while their mammies were working in the field."

When the sale was over, then came the separation and

"O, deep was the anguish of that slave mother's heart,
When called from her darlings for ever to part;
The poor mourning mother of reason bereft,
Soon ended her sorrows and sank cold in death."

Antoinette, the flower of the family, a girl who was much beloved by all who knew her, for her Christ-like piety, dignity of manner, as well as her great talents and extreme beauty, was bought by an uneducated and drunken salve-dealer.

I cannot give a more correct description of the scene, when she was called from her brother to the stand, than will be found in the following lines

"Why stands she near the auction stand?
That girl so young and fair;
What brings her to this dismal place?
Why stands she weeping there?

Why does she raise that bitter cry?
Why hangs her head with shame,
As now the auctioneer's rough voice
So rudely calls her name!

But see! she grasps a manly hand,
And in a voice so low,
As scarcely to be heard, she says,
"My brother, must I go?"

A moment's pause: then, midst a wail
Of agonizing woe,
His answer falls upon the ear,
"Yes, sister, you must go!

No longer can my arm defend,
No longer can I save
My sister from the horrid fate
That waits her as a SLAVE!"

Blush, Christian, blush! for e'en the dark
Untutored heathen see
Thy inconsistency, and lo!
They scorn thy God, and thee!"

The low trader said to a kind lady who wished to purchase Antoinette out of his hands, "I reckon I'll not sell the smart critter for ten thousand dollars; I always wanted her for my own use." The lady, wishing to remonstrate with him, commenced by saying, "You should remember, Sir, that there is a just God." Hoskens not understanding Mrs. Huston, interrupted her by saying, "I does, and guess its monstrous kind an' him to send such likely niggers for our convenience." Mrs. Huston, finding that a long course of reckless wickedness, drunkenness, and vice, had destroyed in Hoskens every noble impulse, left him.

Antoinette, a poor girl, also seeing that there was no help for her, became frantic. I can never forget her cries of despair, when Hoskens gave the order for her to be taken to his house and locked in an upper room. On Hoskens entering the apartment, in a state of intoxication, a fearful struggle ensued. The brave Antoinette broke loose from him, pitched herself head foremost through the window and fell upon the pavement below.

Her bruised but unpolluted body was soon picked up restoratives brought, doctor called in but, alas! it was too late: her pure and noble spirit had fled away to be at rest in those realms of endless bliss, "where the wicked cease from troubling, and the weary are at rest."

Antoinette like many other noble women who are deprived of liberty, still.

"Holds something sacred, something undefiled;
Some pledge and keepsake of their higher nature.
And, like the diamond in the dark, retains
Some quenchless gleam of the celestial light."

On Hoskens fully realizing the fact that his victim was no more, he exclaimed "By thunder I am a used-up man!" The sudden disappointment, and the loss of two thousand dollars, was more than he could endure so he drank more than ever, and in a short time died, raving mad with delirium tremens.

The villain Slator said to Mrs. Huston, the kind lady who endeavoured to purchase Antoinette from Hoskens, "Nobody needn't talk to me 'bout buying them ar likely niggers, for I'm not going to sell them." "But Mary is rather delicate," said Mrs. Huston, "and, being unaccustomed to hard work, cannot do you much service on a plantation." "I don't want her for the field," replied Slator, "but for another purpose." Mrs. Huston understood what this meant, and instantly exclaimed, "Oh, but she is your cousin!" "The devil she is!" said Slator and added, "Do you mean to insult me, Madam, by saying that I am related to niggers?" "No," replied Mrs. Huston, "I do not wish to offend you, Sir. But wasn't Mr. Slator, Mary's father, your uncle?" "Yes, I calculate he was," said Slator; "but I want you and everybody to understand that I'm no kin to his niggers." "Oh, very well," said Mrs. Huston; adding, "Now what will you take for the poor girl?" "Nothing," he replied "for, as I said before, I'm not going to sell, so you needn't trouble yourself no more. If the critter behaves herself, I'll do as well by her as any man."

Slator spoke up boldly, but his manner and sheepish look clearly indicated that

"His heart within him was at strife
With such accursed gains;
For he knew whose passions gave her life,
Whose blood ran in her veins."

"The monster led her from the door,
He led her by the hand,
To be his slave and paramour
In a strange and distant land!"

Poor Frank and his sister were handcuffed together and confined in prison. Their dear little twin brother and sister were sold and taken where they knew not. But it often happens that misfortune causes those whom we counted dearest to shrink away; while it makes friends of those whom we least expected to take any interest in our affairs. Among the latter class Frank found two comparatively new but faithful friends to watch the gloomy paths of the unhappy little twins.

In a day or two after the sale, Slator had two fast horses put to a large light van and placed in it a good many small but valuable things belonging to the distressed family. He also took with him Frank and Mary, as well as all the money for the spoil; and after treating all his low friends and bystanders, and drinking deeply himself, he started in high glee for his home in South Carolina. But they had not proceeded many miles, before Frank and his sister discovered that Slator was too drunk to drive. But he, like most tipsy men, thought he was all right; and as he had with him some of the ruined family's best brandy and wine, such as he had not been accustomed to, and being a thirsty soul, he drank till the reins fell from his fingers, and in attempting to catch them he tumbled out of the vehicle and was unable to get up. Frank and Mary there and then contrived a plan by which to escape. As they were still handcuffed by one wrist each, they alighted, took from the drunken assassin's pocket the key, undid the iron bracelets, and placed them upon Slator, who was better fitted to wear such ornaments. As the demon lay unconscious of what was taking place, Frank and Mary took from him the large sum of money that was realized at the sale, as well as that which Slator had so very meanly obtained from their poor mother. They then dragged him into the woods, tied him to a tree, and left the inebriated robber to shift for himself, while they made good their escape to Savannah. The fugitives being white, of course no one suspected that they were slaves.

Slator was not able to call anyone to his rescue till late the next day and as there were no railroads in that part of the country at that time, it was not until late the following day that Slator was able to get a party to join him for the chase. A person informed

Slator that he had met a man and woman, in a trap, answering to the description of those whom he had lost, driving furiously towards Savannah. So, Slator and several slave-hunters on horseback started off in full tilt, with their bloodhounds, in pursuit of Frank and Mary.

On arriving at Savannah, the hunters found that the fugitives had sold the horses and trap, and embarked as free white persons, for New York. Slator's disappointment and rascality so preyed upon his base mind, that he, like Judas, went and hanged himself.

As soon as Frank and Mary were safe, they endeavoured to redeem their good mother. But alas! she was gone; she had passed on to the realm of spirit life.

In due time Frank learned from his friends in Georgia where his little brother and sister dwelt. So, he wrote at once to purchase them, but the persons with whom they lived would not sell them. After failing in several attempts to buy them, Frank cultivated large whiskers and moustachios, cut off his hair, put on a wig and glasses, and went down as a white man, and stopped in the neighbourhood where his sister was and after seeing her and also his little brother, arrangements were made for them to meet at a particular place on a Sunday, which they did, and got safely off.

I saw Frank myself, when he came for the little twins. Though I was then quite a lad, I well remember being highly delighted by hearing him tell how nicely he and Mary had served Slator.

Frank had so completely disguised or changed his appearance that his little sister did not know him and would not speak till he showed their mother's likeness; the sight of which melted her to tears, for she knew the face. Frank might have said to her,

"'O, Emma! O, my sister, speak to me!
Dost thou not know me, that I am thy brother?
Come to me, little Emma, thou shalt dwell
With me henceforth, and know no care or want.'
Emma was silent for a space, as if
'It were hard to summon up a human voice."
Frank and Mary's mother was my wife's own
dear aunt.

After this great diversion from our narrative, which I hope, dear reader, you will excuse, I shall return at once to it.

My wife was torn from her mother's embrace in childhood and taken to a distant part of the country. She had seen so many other children separated from their parents in this cruel manner, that the mere thought of her ever becoming the mother of a child, to linger out a miserable existence under the wretched system of American slavery, appeared to fill her very soul with horror; and as she had taken what I felt to be an important view of her condition, I did not, at first, press the marriage, but agreed to assist her in trying to devise some plan by which we might escape from our unhappy condition, and then be married.

We thought of plan after plan, but they all seemed crowded with insurmountable difficulties. We knew it was unlawful for any public conveyance to take us as passengers, without our master's consent. We were also perfectly aware of the startling fact, that had we left without this consent the professional slave-hunters would have soon had their ferocious bloodhounds baying on our track, and in a short time we should have been dragged back to slavery, not to fill the more favourable situations which we had just left, but to be separated for life, and put to the very meanest and most laborious drudgery; or else have been tortured to death as examples, in order to strike terror into the hearts of others, and thereby pre- vent them from even attempting to escape from their cruel taskmasters. It is a fact worthy of remark that nothing seems to give the slaveholders so much pleasure as the catching and torturing of fugitives. They had much rather take the keen and poisonous lash, and with it cut their poor trembling victims to atoms, than allow one of them to escape to a free country and expose the infamous system from which he fled.

The greatest excitement prevails at a slave-hunt. The slaveholders and their hired ruffians appear to take more pleasure in this inhuman pursuit than English sportsmen do in chasing a fox or a stag. Therefore, knowing what we should have been compelled to suffer, if caught and taken back, we were more than anxious to hit upon a plan that would lead us safely to a land of liberty.

But, after puzzling our brains for years, we were reluctantly driven to the sad conclusion, that it was almost impossible to escape from slavery in Georgia, and travel 1,000 miles across the slave States. We therefore resolved to get the consent of our owners, be married, settle down in slavery and endeavour to make ourselves as comfortable as possible under that system but at the same time ever to keep our dim eyes steadily fixed upon the glimmering hope of liberty, and earnestly pray God mercifully to assist us to escape from our unjust thraldom.

We were married, and prayed and toiled on till December 1848, at which time (as I have stated) a plan suggested itself that proved quite successful and in eight days after it was first thought of, we were free from the horrible trammels of slavery and glorifying God who had brought us safely out of a land of bondage.

Knowing that slaveholders have the privilege of taking their slaves to any part of the country they think proper, it occurred to me that, as my wife was nearly white, I might get her to disguise herself as an invalid gentleman, and assume to be my master, while I could attend as his slave, and that in this manner we might effect our escape. After I thought of the plan, I suggested it to my wife but at first, she shrank from the idea. She thought it was almost impossible for her to assume that disguise and travel a distance of 1,000 miles across the slave States. However, on the other hand, she also thought of her condition. She saw that the laws under which we lived did not recognize her to be a woman but a mere chattel, to be bought and sold, or otherwise dealt with as her owner might see fit. Therefore, the more she contemplated her helpless condition, the more anxious she was to escape from it. So, she said, "I think it is almost too much for us to undertake however, I feel that God is on our side and with his assistance, notwithstanding all the difficulties, we shall be able to succeed. Therefore, if you will purchase the disguise, I will try to carry out the plan."

But after I decided to purchase the disguise, I was afraid to go to anyone to ask him to sell me the articles. It is unlawful in Georgia for a white man to trade with slaves without the master's consent. But, notwithstanding this, many persons will sell a slave any article that he can get the money to buy. Not that they sympathize with the slave but merely because his testimony is not admitted in court against a free white person.

Therefore, with little difficulty I went to different parts of the town, at odd times and purchased things piece by piece, (except the trowsers which she found necessary to make) and took them home to the house where my wife resided. She is being a ladies' maid and a favourite slave in the family, was allowed a little room to herself and amongst other pieces of furniture which I had made in my overtime, was a chest of drawers so when I took the articles home, she locked them up carefully in these drawers. No one about the premises knew that she had anything of the kind. So, when we fancied, we had everything ready the time was fixed for the flight. But we knew it would not be good to start off without first getting our master's consent to be away for a few days. Had we left without this, they would soon have sent us back into slavery, and probably we should never have got another fair opportunity of even attempting to escape.

Some of the best slaveholders will sometimes give their favourite slaves a few days' holiday at Christmas time; so, after no little amount of perseverance on my wife's part, she obtained a pass from her mistress, allowing her to be away for a few days. The cabinetmaker with whom I worked gave me a similar paper, but said that he needed my services very much, and wished me to return as soon as the time granted was up. I thanked him kindly but somehow, I have not been able to make it convenient to return yet; and, as the free air of good old England agrees so well with my wife and our dear little ones, as well as with myself, it is not at all likely we shall return at present to the "peculiar institution" of chains and stripes.

On reaching my wife's cottage she handed me her pass, and I showed mine, but at that time neither of us were able to read it. It is not only unlawful for slaves to be taught to read, but in some of the States there are heavy penalties attached, such as fines and imprisonment, which will be vigorously enforced upon anyone who is humane enough to violate the so-called law.

The following case will serve to show how people are treated in the most enlightened slaveholding community.

"INDICTMENT.

COMMONWEALTH OF VIRGINIA,} In the Circuit

NORFOLK COUNTY, ss.} Court. The Grand Jurors empannelled in the body of the said County on their oath present, that Margaret Doug- lass, being an evil disposed person, not having the fear of God before her eyes, but moved and instigated by the devil, wickedly, maliciously, and feloniously, on the fourth day of July, in the year of our Lord one thousand eight hundred and fifty- four, at Norfolk, in said County, did teach a certain black girl named Kate to read in the Bible, to the great displeasure of Almighty God, to the pernicious example of others in like case offending, contrary to the form of the statute in such case made and provided, and against the peace and dignity of the Commonwealth of Virginia.

"VICTOR VAGABOND, Prosecuting Attorney."

"On this indictment Mrs. Douglass was arraigned as a necessary matter of form, tried, found guilty of course; and Judge Scalaway, before whom she was tried, having consulted with Dr. Adams, ordered the sheriff to place Mrs. Douglass in the prisoner's box, when he addressed her as follows: 'Margaret Douglass, stand up. You are guilty of one of the vilest crimes that ever-disgraced society and the jury have found you so. You have taught a slave girl to read in the Bible. No enlightened society can exist where such offences go unpunished. The Court, in your case, do not feel for you one solitary ray of sympathy and they will inflict on you the utmost penalty of the law. In any other civilized country, you would have paid the forfeit of your crime with your life, and the Court have only to regret that such is not the law in this country. The sentence for your offence is that you be imprisoned one month in the county jail and that you pay the costs of this prosecution. Sheriff, remove the prisoner to jail.' On the publication of these proceedings, the Doctor of Divinity preached each a sermon on the necessity of obeying the laws; the New York Observer noticed with much pious gladness a revival of religion on Dr. Smith's plantation in Georgia, among his slaves; while the Journal of Commerce commended this political preaching of the Doctor of Divinity because it favoured slavery. Let us do nothing to offend our Southern brethren."

However, at first, we were highly delighted at the idea of having gained permission to be absent for a few days but when the thought flashed across my wife's mind, that it was customary for travellers to register their names in the visitors' book at hotels, as well as in the clearance or Custom-house book at Charleston, South Carolina it made our spirits droop within us.

So, while sitting in our little room upon the verge of despair, all at once my wife raised her head, and with a smile upon her face, which was a moment before bathed in tears, said, "I think I have it!" I asked what it was. She said, "I think I can make a poultice and bind up my right hand in a sling, and with propriety ask the officers to register my name for me." I thought that would do.

It then occurred to her that the smoothness of her face might betray her, so she decided to make another poultice, and put it in a white handkerchief to be worn under the chin, up the cheeks, and to tie over the head. This nearly hid the expression of the countenance, as well as the beardless chin.

The poultice is left off in the engraving because the likeness could not have been taken well with it on.

My wife, knowing that she would be thrown a good deal into the company of gentlemen, fancied that she could get on better if she had something to go over the eyes so, I went to a shop and bought a pair of green spectacles. This was in the evening.

We sat up all night discussing the plan and making preparations. Just before the time arrived, in the morning, for us to leave, I cut off my wife's hair square at the back of the head and got her to dress in disguise and stand out on the floor. I found that she made a most respectable looking gentleman.

My wife had no ambition whatever to assume this disguise, and would not have done so had it been possible to have obtained our liberty by more simple means; but we knew it was not customary in the South for ladies to travel with male servants; and therefore, notwithstanding my wife's fair complexion, it would have been a very difficult task for her to have come off as a free white lady, with me as her slave; in fact, her not being able to write would have made this quite impossible. We knew that no public conveyance would take us, or any other slave, as a passenger, without our master's consent. This consent could never be obtained to pass into a free State. My wife's being muffled in the poultices, &c., furnished a plausible excuse for avoiding general conversation, of which most Yankee travellers are passionately fond.

There are a large number of free negroes residing in the southern States but in Georgia (and I believe in all the slave States,) every coloured person's complexion is prima facie evidence of his being a slave; and the lowest villain in the country, should he be a white man, has the legal power to arrest, and question, in the most inquisitorial and insulting manner, any coloured person, male or female, that he may find at large, particularly at night and on Sundays, without a written pass, signed by the master or someone in authority or stamped free papers, certifying that the person is the rightful owner of himself.

If the coloured person refuses to answer questions put to him, he may be beaten, and his defending himself against this attack makes him an outlaw and if he be killed on the spot, the murderer will be exempted from all blame but after the coloured person has answered the questions put to him, in a most humble and pointed manner, he may then be taken to prison and should it turn out, after further examination, that he was caught where he had no permission or legal right to be and that he has not given what they term a satisfactory account of himself, the master will have to pay a fine. On his refusing to do this, the poor slave may be legally and severely flogged by public officers. Should the prisoner prove to be a free man, he is most likely to be both whipped and fined.

The great majority of slaveholders hate this class of persons with a hatred that can only be equalled by the condemned spirits of the infernal regions. They have no mercy upon, nor sympathy for, any negro whom they cannot enslave. They say that God made the black man to be a slave for the white and act as though they really believed that all free persons of colour are in open rebellion to a direct command from heaven, and that they (the whites) are God's chosen agents to pour out upon them unlimited vengeance. For instance, a Bill has been introduced in the Tennessee Legislature to prevent free negroes from travelling on the rail- roads in that State. It has passed the first reading. The bill provides that the President who shall permit a free negro to travel on any road within the jurisdiction of the State under his supervision shall pay a fine of 500 dollars; any conductor permitting a violation of the Act shall pay 250 dollars; provided such free negro is not under the control of a free white citizen of Tennessee, who will vouch for the character of said free negro in a penal bond of one thousand dollars. The State of Arkansas has passed a law to banish all free negroes from its bounds, and it came into effect on the 1st day of January 1860. Every free negro found there after that date will be liable to be sold into slavery, the crime of freedom being unpardonable. The Missouri Senate has before it a bill providing that all free negroes above the age of eighteen years who shall be found in the State after September 1860, shall be sold into slavery; and that all such negroes as shall enter the State after September 1861, and remain there twenty-four hours, shall also be sold into slavery forever. Mississippi, Kentucky, and Georgia, and in fact, I believe, all the slave States, are legislating in the same manner. Thus, the slaveholders make it almost im- possible for free persons of colour to get out of the slave States, in order that they may sell them into slavery if they don't go. If no white persons travelled upon railroads except those who could get someone to vouch for their character in a penal bond of one thousand dollars, the railroad companies would soon go to the "wall." Such mean legislation is too low for comment therefore I leave the villainous acts to speak for themselves.

But the Dred Scott decision is the crowning act of infamous Yankee legislation. The Supreme Court, the highest tribunal of the Republic, composed of nine Judge Jeffries's, chosen both from the free and slave States, has decided that no coloured person, or persons of African extraction, can ever become a citizen of the United States, or have any rights which white men are bound to respect. That is to say, in the opinion of this Court, robbery, rape and murder are not crimes when committed by a white upon a coloured person.

Judges who will sneak from their high and honourable position down into the lowest depths of human depravity, and scrape up a decision like this, are wholly unworthy of the confidence of any people. I believe such men would, if they had the power, and were it to their temporal interest, sell their country's independence, and barter away every man's birthright for a mess of pottage. Well, may Thomas Campbell say.

United States, your banner wears,
Two emblems, one of fame,
Alas, the other that it bears
Reminds us of your shame!
The white man's liberty in types
Stands blazoned by your stars;
But what's the meaning of your stripes?
They mean your Negro-scars.

When the time had arrived for us to start, we blew out the lights, knelt down, and prayed to our Heavenly Father mercifully to assist us, as he did his people of old, to escape from cruel bondage; and we shall ever feel that God heard and answered our prayer. Had we not been sustained by a kind, and I sometimes think special, providence, we could never have overcome the mountainous difficulties which I am now about to describe.

After this we rose and stood for a few moments in breathless silence, we were afraid that someone might have been about the cottage listening and watching our movements. So, I took my wife by the hand, stepped softly to the door, raised the latch, drew it open, and peeped out. Though there were trees all around the house, yet the foliage scarcely moved; in fact, everything appeared to be as still as death. I then whispered to my wife, "Come, my dear, let us make a desperate leap for liberty!" But poor thing, she shrank back, in a state of trepidation. I turned and asked what was the matter; she made no reply, but burst into violent sobs, and threw her head upon my breast. This appeared to touch my very heart, it caused me to enter into her feelings more fully than ever. We both saw the many mountainous difficulties that rose one after the other before our view and knew far too well what our sad fate would have been, were we caught and forced back into our slavish den. Therefore, on my wife's fully realizing the solemn fact that we had to take our lives, as it were, in our hands, and contest every inch of the thousand miles of slave territory over which we had to pass, it made her heart almost sink within her and had I known them at that time, I would have repeated the following encouraging lines, which may not be out of place here,

"The hill, though high, I covet to ascend,
The difficulty will not me offend;
For I perceive the way to life lies here:
Come, pluck up heart, let's neither faint nor fear;
Better, though difficult, the right way to go,
Than wrong, though easy, where the end is woe."

However, the sobbing was soon over, and after a few moments of silent prayer she recovered her self-possession, and said, "Come, William, it is getting late, so now let us venture upon our perilous journey."

We then opened the door and stepped as softly out as "moonlight upon the water." I locked the door with my own key, which I now have before me, and tiptoed across the yard into the street. I say tiptoed, because we were like persons near a tottering avalanche, afraid to move or even breathe freely, for fear the sleeping tyrants should be aroused, and come down upon us with double vengeance, for daring to attempt to escape in the manner which we contemplated.

We shook hands, said farewell, and started in different directions for the railway station. I took the nearest possible way to the train, for fear I should be recognized by someone, and got into the negro car in which I knew I should have to ride but my Master (as I will now call my wife) took a longer way round and only arrived there with the bulk of the passengers. He obtained a ticket for himself and one for his slave to Savannah, the first port, which was about two hundred miles off. My master then had the luggage stowed away, and stepped into one of the best carriages.

But just before the train moved off I peeped through the window, and, to my great astonishment, I saw the cabinet-maker with whom I had worked so long, on the platform. He stepped up to the ticket-seller and asked some questions and then commenced looking rapidly through the passengers, and into the carriages. Fully believing that we were caught, I shrank into a corner, turned my face from the door and expected in a moment to be dragged out. The cabinetmaker looked into my master's carriage but did not know him in his new attire, and, as God would have it, before he reached mine the bell rang, and the train moved off.

I have heard since that the cabinetmaker had a pre-sentiment that we were about to "make tracks for parts unknown;" but, not seeing me, his suspicions vanished, until he received the startling intelligence that we had arrived freely in a free State.

As soon as the train had left the platform, my master looked round in the carriage, and was terror-stricken to find a Mr. Cray, an old friend of my wife's master, who dined with the family the day before, and knew my wife from childhood sitting on the same seat.

The doors of the American railway carriages are at the ends. The passengers walk up the aisle, and take seats on either side; and as my master was engaged in looking out of the window, he did not see who came in.

My master's first impression, after seeing Mr. Cray, was, that he was there for the purpose of securing him. However, my master thought it was not wise to give any information respecting himself and for fear that Mr. Cray might draw him into conversation and recognise his voice, my master resolved to feign deafness as the only means of self-defence.

After a little while, Mr. Cray said to my master, "It is a very fine morning, sir." The latter took no notice, but kept looking out of the window. Mr. Cray soon repeated this remark, in a little louder tone, but my master remained as before. This indifference attracted the attention of the passengers near, one of whom laughed out. This, I suppose, annoyed the old gentleman; so he said, "I will make him hear;" and in a loud tone of voice repeated, "It is a very fine morning, sir."

My master turned his head, and with a polite bow said, "Yes," and commenced looking out of the window again.

One of the gentlemen remarked that it was a very great deprivation to be deaf. "Yes," replied Mr. Cray, "and I shall not trouble that fellow anymore." This enabled my master to breathe a little easier, and to feel that Mr. Cray was not his pursuer after all.

The gentlemen then turned the conversation upon the three great topics of discussion in first- class circles in Georgia, namely, Niggers, Cotton, and the Abolitionists.

My master had often heard of abolitionists, but in such a connection as to cause him to think that they were a fearful kind of wild animal. But he was highly delighted to learn, from the gentlemen's conversation, that the abolitionists were persons who were opposed to oppression and therefore, in his opinion, not the lowest, but the very highest, of God's creatures.

Without the slightest objection on my master's part, the gentlemen left the carriage at Gordon, for Milledgeville (the capital of the State).

We arrived at Savannah early in the evening, and got into an omnibus, which stopped at the hotel for the passengers to take tea. I stepped into the house and brought my master something on a tray to the omnibus, which took us in due time to the steamer, which was bound for Charleston, South Carolina.

Soon after going on board, my master turned in; and as the captain and some of the passengers seemed to think this strange, and also questioned me respecting him, my master thought I had better get out the flannels and opodeldoc which we had prepared for the rheumatism, warm them quickly by the stove in the gentleman's saloon and bring them to his berth. We did this as an excuse for my master's retiring to bed so early.

While at the stove one of the passengers said to me, "Buck, what have you got there?" "Opodel-doc, sir," I replied. "I should think it's opo-devil," said a lanky swell, who was leaning back in a chair with his heels upon the back of another and chewing tobacco as if for a wager; "it stinks enough to kill or cure twenty men. Away with it, or I reckon I will throw it overboard!"

It was by this time warm enough, so I took it to my master's berth, remained there a little while, and then went on deck and asked the steward where I was to sleep. He said there was no place provided for coloured passengers, whether slave or free. So, I paced the deck till a late hour, then mounted some cotton bags, in a warm place near the funnel, sat there till morning, and then went and assisted my master to get ready for breakfast.

He was seated at the right hand of the captain, who, together with all the passengers, inquired very kindly after his health. As my master had one hand in a sling, it was my duty to carve his food. But when I went out the captain said, "You have a very attentive boy Sir, but you had better watch him like a hawk when you get on to the North. He seems very well here but he may act quite differently there. I know several gentlemen who have lost their valuable niggers among them d——d cut-throat abolitionists."

Before my master could speak, a rough slave-dealer, who was sitting opposite, with both elbows on the table, and with a large piece of broiled fowl in his fingers, shook his head with emphasis, and in a deep Yankee tone, forced through his crowded mouth the words, "Sound doctrine, captain, very sound." He then dropped the chicken into the plate, leant back, placed his thumbs in the armholes of his fancy waistcoat, and continued, "I would not take a nigger to the North under no consideration. I have had a deal to do with niggers in my time, but I never saw one who ever had his heel upon free soil that was worth a d——n." "Now stranger," addressing my master, "if you have made up your mind to sell that ere nigger, I am your man; just mention your price, and if it isn't out of the way, I will pay for him on this board with hard silver dollars." This hard-featured, bristly-bearded, wire-headed, red-eyed monster, staring at my master as the serpent did at Eve, said, "What do you say, stranger?" He replied, "I don't wish to sell, sir; I cannot get on well with- out him."

"You will have to get on without him if you take him to the North," continued this man; "for I can tell ye, stranger, as a friend, I am an older cove than you, I have seen lots of this ere world, and I reckon I have had more dealings with niggers than any man living or dead. I was once employed by General Wade Hampton, for ten years, in doing nothing but breaking them in and everybody knows that the General would not have a man that didn't understand his business. So, I tell ye, stranger, again, you had better sell, and let me take him down to Orleans. He will do you no good if you take him across Mason's and Dixon's line; he is a keen nigger, and I can see from the cut of his eye that he is certain to run away." My master said, "I think not, sir; I have great confidence in his fidelity." "Fideviil," indignantly said the dealer, as his fist came down upon the edge of the saucer and upset a cup of hot coffee in a gentleman's lap. (As the scalded man jumped up the trader quietly said, "Don't disturb yourself, neighbour, accidents will happen in the best of families.") "It always makes me mad to hear a man talking about fidelity in niggers. There isn't a d——d one on them who wouldn't cut sticks, if he had half a chance."

By this time, we were near Charleston; my master thanked the captain for his advice, and they all withdrew and went on deck, where the trader fancied, he became quite eloquent. He drew a crowd around him and with emphasis said, "Cap'en, if I was the President of this mighty United States of America, the greatest and freest country under the whole universe, I would never let no man, I don't care who he is, take a nigger into the North and bring him back here, filled to the brim, as he is sure to be, with d——d abolition vices, to taint all quiet niggers with the hellish spirit of running away. These air, cap'en, my flat-footed, every day, right up and down sentiments, and as this is a free country, cap'en, I don't care who hears them; for I am a Southern man, every inch on me to the backbone." "Good!" said an insignificant-looking individual of the slave-dealer stamp. "Three cheers for John C. Calhoun and the whole fair sunny South!" added the trader. So off went their hats and outburst a terrific roar of irregular but continued cheering. My master took no more notice of the dealer. He merely said to the captain that the air on deck was too keen for him, and he would therefore return to the cabin.

While the trader was in the zenith of his eloquence, he might as well have said, as one of his kits did, at a great Filibustering meeting, that "When the great American Eagle gets one of his mighty claws upon Canada and the other into South America, and his glorious and starry wings of liberty extending from the Atlantic to the Pacific, oh! then, where will England be, ye gentlemen? I tell ye, she will only serve as a pocket- handkerchief for Jonathan to wipe his nose with."

On my master entering the cabin he found at the breakfast table a young southern military officer, with whom he had travelled some distance the previous day.

After passing the usual compliments the conversation turned upon the old subject, niggers.

The officer, who was also travelling with a man- servant, said to my master, "You will excuse me, Sir, for saying I think you are very likely to spoil your boy by saying 'thank you' to him. I assure you, sir, nothing spoils a slave so soon as saying, 'thank you' and 'if you please' to him. The only way to make a nigger toe the mark, and to keep him in his place, is to storm at him like thunder, and keep him trembling like a leaf. Don't you see, when I speak to my Ned, he darts like lightning; and if he didn't, I'd skin him."

Just then the poor dejected slave came in, and the officer swore at him fearfully, merely to teach my master what he called the proper way to treat me.

After he had gone out to get his master's luggage ready, the officer said, "That is the way to speak to them. If every nigger was drilled in this manner, they would be as humble as dogs, and never dare to run away.

The gentleman urged my master not to go to the North for the restoration of his health, but to visit the Warm Springs in Arkansas.

My master said, he thought the air of Philadelphia would suit his complaint best and not only so he thought he could get better advice there.

The boat had now reached the wharf. The officer wished my master a safe and pleasant journey and left the saloon.

There were a large number of people on the quay awaiting the arrival of the steamer: but we were afraid to venture out for fear that someone might recognize me or that they had heard that we were gone and had telegraphed to have us stopped. However, after remaining in the cabin till all the other passengers were gone, we had our luggage placed on a fly, and I took my master by the arm, and with a little difficulty he hobbled on shore, got in and drove off to the best hotel, which John C. Calhoun, and all the other great southern fire-eating statesmen, made their headquarters while in Charleston.

On arriving at the house, the landlord ran out and opened the door but judging from the poultices and green glasses, that my master was an invalid, he took him very tenderly by one arm and ordered his man to take the other.

My master then eased himself out and with their assistance found no trouble in getting up the steps into the hotel. The proprietor made me stand on one side, while he paid my master attention and homage, he thought a gentleman of his high position merited.

My master asked for a bedroom. The servant was ordered to show a good one, into which we helped him. The servant returned. My master then handed me the bandages, I took them down- stairs in great haste, and told the landlord my master wanted two hot poultices as quickly as possible. He rang the bell, the servant came in, to whom he said, "Run to the kitchen and tell the cook to make two hot poultices right off, for there is a gentleman upstairs very badly off indeed!"

In a few minutes the smoking poultices were brought in. I placed them in white handkerchiefs, and hurried upstairs, went into my master's apartment, shut the door, and laid them on the mantelpiece. As he was alone for a little while, he thought he could rest a great deal better with the poultices off. However, it was necessary to have them to complete the remainder of the journey. I then ordered dinner and took my master's boots out to polish them. While doing so I entered into conversation with one of the slaves. I may state here, that on the seacoast of South Carolina and Georgia the slaves speak worse English than in any other part of the country. This is owing to the frequent importation, or smuggling in, of Africans, who mingle with the natives. Consequently, the language cannot properly be called English or African, but a corruption of the two.

The shrewd son of African parents to whom I referred said to me, "Say, brudder, way you come from, and which side you goin day wid dat ar little don up buckra" (white man)?

I replied, "To Philadelphia."

"What!" he exclaimed, with astonishment, "to Philumadelphy?"

"Yes," I said.

"By squash! I wish I was going wid you! I hears um say dat dare's no slave's way over in dem parts; is um so?"

I quietly said, "I have heard the same thing."

"Well," continued he, as he threw down the boot and brush, and, placing his hands in his pockets, strutted across the floor with an air of independence "Gorra Mighty, dem is de parts for Pompey and I hope when you get dare you will stay, and nebber follow dat buckra back to dis hot quarter no more, let him be eber so good."

I thanked him and just as I took the boots up and started off, he caught my hand between his two, and gave it a hearty shake, and, with tears streaming down his cheeks, said:

"God bless you, broder, and may de Lord be wid you. When you gets de freedom and siting under your own wine and fig-tree, don't forget to pray for poor Pompey."

I was afraid to say much to him, but I shall never forget his earnest request, nor fail to do what little I can to release the millions of unhappy bondmen, of whom he was one.

At the proper time my master had the poultices placed on, came down, and seated himself at a table in a very brilliant dining-room, to have his dinner. I had to have something at the same time, in order to be ready for the boat; so they gave me my dinner in an old broken plate, with a rusty knife and fork, and said, "Here, boy, you go in the kitchen." I took it and went out, but did not stay more than a few minutes, because I was in a great hurry to get back to see how the invalid was getting on. On arriving I found two or three servants waiting on him; but as he did not feel able to make a very hearty dinner, he soon finished, paid the bill, and gave the servants each a trifle, which caused one of them to say to me, "Your massa is a big bug" meaning a gentleman of distinction "he is the greatest gentleman dat has been dis way for dis six months." I said, "Yes, he is some pumpkins," meaning the same as "big bug."

When we left Macon, it was our intention to take a steamer at Charleston through to Philadelphia but on arriving there we found that the vessels did not run during the winter and I have no doubt it was well for us they did not; for on the very last voyage the steamer made that we intended to go by, a fugitive was discovered secreted on board, and sent back to slavery. However, as we had also heard of the Overland Mail Route, we were all right. So I ordered a fly to the door, had the luggage placed on; we got in, and drove down to the Custom-house Office, which was near the wharf where we had to obtain tickets, to take a steamer for Wilmington, North Carolina. When we reached the building, I helped my master into the office, which was crowded with passengers. He asked for a ticket for himself and one for his slave to Philadelphia. This caused the principal officer, a very mean-looking, cheese-coloured fellow, who was sitting there to look up at us very suspiciously, and in a fierce tone of voice he said to me, "Boy, do you belong to that gentleman?" I quickly replied, "Yes, sir" (which was quite correct). The tickets were handed out, and as my master was paying for them the chief man said to him, "I wish you to register your name here, sir and also the name of your nigger, and pay a dollar duty on him."

My master paid the dollar and pointing to the hand that was in the poultice, requested the officer to register his name for him. This seemed to offend the "high-bred" South Carolinian. He jumped up, shaking his head and cramming his hands almost through the bottom of his trousers pockets, with a slave-bullying air, said, "I shan't do it."

This attracted the attention of all the passengers. Just then the young military officer with whom my master travelled and conversed on the steamer from Savannah stepped in, somewhat the worse for brandy; he shook hands with my master and pretended to know all about him. He said, "I know his kin (friends) like a book;" and as the officer was known in Charleston, and was going to stop there with friends, the recognition was very much in my master's favor.

The captain of the steamer, a good-looking, jovial fellow, seeing that the gentleman appeared to know my master, and perhaps not wishing to lose us as passengers, said in an off-hand sailor-like manner, "I will register the gentleman's name, and take the responsibility upon myself." He asked my master's name. He said, "William Johnson." The names were put down, I think, "Mr. Johnson and slave." The captain said, "It's all right now, Mr. Johnson." He thanked him kindly and the young officer begged my master to go with him and have something to drink and a cigar but as he had not acquired these accomplishments, he excused himself and we went on board and came off to Wilmington, North Carolina. When the gentleman finds out his mistake, he will, I have no doubt, be careful in future not to pretend to have an intimate acquaintance with an entire stranger. During the voyage the captain said, "It was rather sharp shooting this morning, Mr. Johnson. It was not out of any disrespect to you, sir; but they make it a rule to be very strict at Charleston. I have known families to be detained there with their slaves till reliable information could be received respecting them. If they were not very careful, any d——d abolitionist might take off a lot of valuable niggers."

My master said, "I suppose so," and thanked him again for helping him over the difficulty.

We reached Wilmington the next morning, and took the train for Richmond, Virginia. I have stated that the American railway carriages (or cars, as they are called), are constructed differently to those in England. At one end of some of them, in the South, there is a little apartment with a couch on both sides for the convenience of families and invalids and as they thought my master was very poorly, he was allowed to enter one of these apartments at Petersburg, Virginia, where an old gentleman and two handsome young ladies, his daughters, also got in, and took seats in the same carriage. But before the train started, the gentle- man stepped into my car, and questioned me respecting my master. He wished to know what the matter with him was, where he was from, and where he was going. I told him where he came from and said that he was suffering from a complication of complaints, and was going to Philadelphia, where he thought he could get more suitable advice than in Georgia.

The gentleman said my master could obtain the very best advice in Philadelphia. Which turned out to be quite correct, though he did not receive it from physicians, but from kind abolitionists who understood his case much better. The gentleman also said, "I reckon your master's father hasn't any more such faithful and smart boys as you." "O, yes, sir, he has," I replied, "lots on them." Which was literally true. This seemed all he wished to know. He thanked me, gave me a ten-cent piece, and requested me to be attentive to my good master. I promised that I would do so and have ever since endeavoured to keep my pledge. During the gentleman's absence, the ladies and my master had a little cosy chat. But on his return, he said, "You seem to be very much afflicted, sir." "Yes, sir," replied the gentleman in the poultices. "What seems to be the matter with you, sir; may I be allowed to ask?" "Inflammatory rheumatism, sir." "Oh! that is very bad, sir," said the kind gentleman: "I can sympathize with you; for I know from bitter experience what rheumatism is." If he did, he knew a good deal more than Mr. Johnson.

The gentleman thought my master would feel better if he would lie down and rest himself and as he was anxious to avoid conversation, he at once acted upon this suggestion. The ladies politely rose, took their extra shawls, and made a nice pillow for the invalid's head. My master wore a fashionable cloth cloak, which they took and covered him comfortably on the couch. After he had been lying a little while the ladies, I suppose, thought he was asleep so one of them gave a long sigh, and said, in a quiet fascinating tone, "Papa, he seems to be a very nice young gentleman." But before papa could speak, the other lady quickly said, "Oh! dear me, I never felt so much for a gentleman in my life!" To use an American expression, "they fell in love with the wrong chap."

After my master had been lying a little while he got up, the gentleman assisted him in getting on his cloak, the ladies took their shawls, and soon they were all seated. They then insisted upon Mr. Johnson taking some of their refreshments, which of course he did, out of courtesy to the ladies. All went on enjoying themselves until they reached Richmond, where the ladies and their father left the train. But, before doing so, the good old Virginian gentleman, who appeared to be very pleased with my master, presented him with a recipe, which he said was a perfect cure for inflammatory rheumatism. But the invalid not being able to read it and fearing he should hold it upside down in pretending to do so, thanked the donor kindly, and placed it in his waistcoat pocket. My master's new friend also gave him his card and requested him the next time he travelled that way to show him the kindness to call; adding, "I shall be pleased to see you, and so will my daughters." Mr. Johnson expressed his gratitude for the proffered hospitality and said he should feel glad to call on his return. I have not the slightest doubt that he will fulfil the promise whenever that return takes place. After changing trains, we went on a little beyond Fredericksburg, and took a steamer to Washington.

At Richmond, a stout elderly lady, whose whole demeanour indicated that she belonged (as Mrs. Stowe's Aunt Chloe expresses it) to one of the "firstest families," stepped into the carriage, and took a seat near my master. Seeing me passing quickly along the platform, she sprang up as if taken by a fit and exclaimed, "Bless my soul! there goes my nigger, Ned!"

My master said, "No; that is my boy."

The lady paid no attention to this; she poked her head out of the window, and bawled to me, "You Ned, come to me, sir, you runaway rascal!"

On my looking round she drew her head in, and said to my master, "I beg your pardon, sir, I was sure it was my nigger; I never in my life saw two black pigs more alike than your boy and my Ned."

After the disappointed lady had resumed her seat, and the train had moved off, she closed her eyes, slightly raising her hands, and in a sanctified tone said to my master, "Oh! I hope, sir, your boy will not turn out to be so worthless as my Ned has. Oh! I was as kind to him as if he had been my own son. Oh! sir, it grieves me very much to think that after all I did for him, he should go off without having any cause whatever."

"When did he leave you?" asked Mr. Johnson.

"About eighteen months ago, and I have never seen hair or hide of him since."

"Did he have a wife?" enquired a very respect- able-looking young gentleman, who was sitting near my master and opposite to the lady.

"No, sir; not when he left, though he did have one a little before that. She was very unlike him; she was as good and as faithful a nigger as any one need wish to have. But poor thing! she became so ill that she was unable to do much work so I thought it would be best to sell her, to go to New Orleans, where the climate is nice and warm."

"I suppose she was very glad to go South for the restoration of her health?" said the gentleman.

"No; she was not," replied the lady, "for niggers never know what is best for them. She took on a great deal about leaving Ned and the little nigger; but, as she was so weakly, I let her go."

"Was she good-looking?" asked the young passenger, who was evidently not of the same opinion as the talkative lady, and therefore wished her to tell all she knew.

"Yes; she was very handsome, and much whiter than I am and therefore will have no trouble in getting another husband. I am sure I wish her well. I asked the speculator who bought her to sell her to a good master. Poor thing! she has my prayers, and I know she prays for me. She was a good Christian, and always used to pray for my soul. It was through her earliest prayers," continued the lady, "that I was first led to seek forgiveness of my sins, before I was converted at the great camp-meeting."

This caused the lady to snuffle and to draw from her pocket a richly embroidered handkerchief and apply it to the corner of her eyes. But my master could not see that it was at all soiled.

The silence which prevailed for a few moments was broken by the gentleman's saying, "As your 'July' was such a very good girl, and had served you so faithfully before she lost her health, don't you think it would have been better to have emancipated her?"

"No, indeed I do not!" scornfully exclaimed the lady, as she impatiently crammed the fine handkerchief into a little workbag. "I have no patience with people who set niggers at liberty. It is the very worst thing you can do for them. My dear husband just before he died willed all his niggers free. But I and all our friends knew very well that he was too good a man to have ever thought of doing such an unkind and foolish thing, had he been in his right mind, and, therefore we had the will altered as it should have been in the first place."

"Did you mean, madam," asked my master, "that willing the slaves free was unjust to yourself, or unkind to them?"

"I mean that it was decidedly unkind to the servants themselves. It always seems to me such a cruel thing to turn niggers loose to shift for themselves, when there are so many good masters to take care of them. As for myself," continued the considerate lady, "I thank the Lord my dear husband left me, and my son well provided for. Therefore, I care nothing for the niggers, on my own account, for they are a great deal more trouble than they are worth, I sometimes wish that there was not one of them in the world for the ungrateful wretches are always running away. I have lost no less than ten since my poor husband died. It's ruinous, sir!"

"But as you are well provided for, I suppose you do not feel the loss very much," said the passenger.

"I don't feel it at all," haughtily continued the good soul; "but that is no reason why property should be squandered. If my son and I had the money for those valuable niggers, just see what a great deal of good we could do for the poor, and in sending missionaries abroad to the poor heathen, who have never heard the name of our blessed Redeemer. My dear son who is a good Christian minister has advised me not to worry and send my soul to hell for the sake of niggers but to sell every blessed one of them for what they will fetch and go and live in peace with him in New York. This I have concluded to do. I have just been to Richmond and made arrangements with my agent to make clean work of the forty that are left."

"Your son being a good Christian minister," said the gentleman, "It's strange he did not advise you to let the poor negroes have their liberty and go North."

"It's not at all strange, sir; it's not at all strange. My son knows what's best for the niggers; he has always told me that they were much better off than the free niggers in the North. In fact, I don't believe there are any white labouring people in the world who are as well off as the slaves."

"You are quite mistaken, madam," said the young man. "For instance, my own widowed mother, before she died, emancipated all her slaves, and sent them to Ohio, where they are getting along well. I saw several of them last summer myself."

"Well," replied the lady, "freedom may do for your ma's niggers but it will never do for mine and plague them, they shall never have it; that is the word, with the bark on it."

"If freedom will not do for your slaves," replied the passenger, "I have no doubt your Ned and the other nine negroes will find out their mistake, and return to their old home.

"Blast them!" exclaimed the old lady, with great emphasis, "if I ever get them, I will cook their infernal hash, and tan their accursed black hides well for them! God forgive me," added the old soul, "the niggers will make me lose all my religion!"

By this time the lady had reached her destination. The gentleman got out at the next station beyond. As soon as she was gone, the young Southerner said to my master, "What a d——d shame it is for that old whining hypocritical humbug to cheat the poor negroes out of their liberty! If she has religion, may the devil prevent me from ever being converted!"

For the purpose of somewhat disguising myself, I bought and wore a very good second-hand white beaver, an article which I had never indulged in before. So just before we arrived at Washington, an uncouth planter, who had been watching me very closely, said to my master, "I reckon, stranger, you are 'SPILING' that ere nigger of your, by letting him wear such a devilish fine hat. Just look at the quality on it; the President couldn't wear a better. I should just like to go and kick it overboard." His friend touched him, and said, "Don't speak so to a gentleman." "Why not?" exclaimed the fellow. He grated his short teeth, which appeared to be nearly worn away by the incessant chewing of tobacco and said, "It always makes me itch all over, from head to toe, to get hold of every d——d nigger I see dressed like a white man. Washington is run away with spiled and free niggers. If I had my way I would sell every d——d rascal of them way down South, where the devil would be whipped out on them."

This man's fierce manner made my master feel rather nervous, and therefore he thought the less he said the better, so he walked off without making any reply. In a few minutes we landed at Washington, where we took a conveyance and hurried off to the train for Baltimore.

We left our cottage on Wednesday morning, the 21st of December 1848, and arrived at Baltimore, Saturday evening, the 24th (Christmas Eve). Baltimore was the last slave port of any note at which we stopped.

On arriving there we felt more anxious than ever, because we did not know what that last dark night would bring forth. It is true we were near the goal, but our poor hearts were still as if tossed at sea; and, as there was another great and dangerous bar to pass, we were afraid our liberties would be wrecked, and, like the ill-fated Royal Charter, go down for ever just off the place we longed to reach.

They are particularly watchful at Baltimore to prevent slaves from escaping into Pennsylvania, which is a free State. After I had seen my master into one of the best carriages, and was just about to step into mine, an officer, a full-blooded Yankee of the lower order, saw me. He came quickly up and tapped me on the shoulder, said in his unmistakable native twang, together with no little dis- play of his authority, "Where are you going, boy?" "To Philadelphia, sir," I humbly replied. "Well, what are you going there for?" "I am travelling with my master, who is in the next carriage, sir." "Well, I calculate you had better get him out; and be mighty quick about it, because the train will soon be starting. It is against my rules to let any man take a slave past here, unless he can satisfy them in the office that he has a right to take him along."

The officer then passed on and left me standing upon the platform, with my anxious heart apparently palpitating in the throat. At first, I scarcely knew which way to turn. But it soon occurred to me that the good God, who had been with us thus far, would not forsake us at the eleventh hour. So, with renewed hope I stepped into my master's carriage, to inform him of the difficulty. I found him sitting at the farther end, quite alone. As soon as he looked up and saw me, he smiled. I also tried to wear a cheerful countenance, in order to break the shock of the sad news. I knew what made him smile. He was aware that if we were fortunate, we should reach our destination at five o'clock the next morning, and this made it the more painful to communicate what the officer had said; but, as there was no time to lose, I went up to him and asked him how he felt. He said, "Much better," and that he thanked God we were getting on so nicely. I then said we were not getting on quite so well as we had anticipated. He anxiously and quickly asked what the matter was. I told him. He started as if struck by lightning, and exclaimed, "Good Heavens! William, is it possible that we are, after all, doomed to hopeless bondage?" I could say nothing, my heart was too full to speak, for at first, I did not know what to do. However, we knew it would never do to turn back to the "City of Destruction," like Bunyan's Mistrust and Timorous, because they saw lions in the narrow way after ascending the hill Difficulty but press on, like noble Christian and Hopeful, to the great city in which dwelt a few "shining ones." So, after a few moments, I did all I could to encourage my companion and we stepped out and made for the office but how or where my master obtained sufficient courage to face the tyrants who had power to blast all we held dear, heaven only knows! Queen Elizabeth could not have been more terror-stricken, on being forced to land at the traitors' gate leading to the Tower, than we were on entering that office. We felt that our very existence was at stake, and that we must either sink or swim. But, as God was our present and mighty helper in this as well as in all former trials, we were able to keep our heads up and press forwards.

On entering the room, we found the principal man, to whom my master said, "Do you wish to see me, sir?" "Yes," said this eagle-eyed officer; and he added, "It is against our rules, sir, to allow any person to take a slave out of Baltimore into Philadelphia, unless he can satisfy us that he has a right to take him along." "Why is that?" asked my master, with more firmness than could be expected. "Because, sir," continued he, in a voice and manner that almost chilled our blood, "if we should suffer any gentleman to take a slave past here into Philadelphia and should the gentleman with whom the slave might be travelling turn out not to be his rightful owner; and should the proper master come and prove that his slave escaped on our road, we shall have him to pay for and therefore, we cannot let any slave pass here without receiving security to show and to satisfy us, that it is all right."

This conversation attracted the attention of the large number of bustling passengers. After the officer had finished, a few of them said, "Chit, chit, chit;" not because they thought we were slaves endeavouring to escape but merely because they thought my master was a slaveholder and invalid gentleman, and therefore it was wrong to detain him. The officer, observing that the passengers sympathized with my master, asked him if he was not acquainted with some gentleman in Baltimore that he could get to endorse for him, to show that I was his property, and that he had a right to take me off. He said, "No;" and added, "I bought tickets in Charleston to pass us through to Philadelphia and therefore you have no right to detain us here." "Well, sir," said the man, indignantly, "right or no right, we shan't let you go." These sharp words fell upon our anxious hearts like the crack of doom and made us feel that hope only smiles to deceive.

For a few moments perfect silence prevailed. My master looked at me, and I at him, but neither of us dared to speak a word, for fear of making some blunder that would tend to our detection. We knew that the officers had power to throw us into prison, and if they had done so we must have been detected and driven back, like the vilest felons, to a life of slavery, which we dreaded far more than sudden death.

We felt as though we had come into deep waters and were about being overwhelmed, and that the slightest mistake would clip asunder the last brittle thread of hope by which we were suspended and let us down for ever into the dark and horrible pit of misery and degradation from which we were straining every nerve to escape. While our hearts were crying lustily unto Him who is ever ready and able to save, the conductor of the train that we had just left stepped in. The officer asked if we came by train with him from Washington; he said we did and left the room. Just then the bell rang for the train to leave; and had it been the sudden shock of an earthquake it could not have given us a greater thrill. The sound of the bell caused every eye to flash with apparent interest, and to be more steadily fixed upon us than before. But, as God would have it, the officer all at once thrust his fingers through his hair, and in a state of great agitation said, "I really don't know what to do; I calculate it is all right." He then told the clerk to run and tell the conductor to "let this gentleman and slave pass;" adding, "As he is not well, it is a pity to stop him here. We will let him go." My master thanked him and stepped out and hobbled across the platform as quickly as possible. I tumbled him unceremoniously into one of the best carriages and leaped into mine just as the train was gliding off towards our happy destination.

We thought of this plan about four days before we left Macon; and as we had our daily employment to attend to, we only saw each other at night. So, we sat up the four long nights talking over the plan and making preparations.

We had also been four days on the journey; and as we travelled night and day, we got very limited opportunities for sleeping. I believe nothing in the world could have kept us awake so long but for the intense excitement produced by the fear of being retaken on the one hand and the bright anticipation of liberty on the other.

We left Baltimore about eight o'clock in the evening and not being aware of a stopping place of any consequence between there and Philadelphia and also knowing that if we were fortunate we should be in the latter place early the next morning, I thought I might indulge in a few minutes' sleep in the car; but I, like Bunyan's Christian in the arbour, went to sleep at the wrong time, and took too long a nap. So, when the train reached Havre de Grace, all the first-class passengers had to get out of the carriages and into a ferryboat, to be ferried across the Susquehanna river, and take the train on the opposite side.

The road was constructed so as to be raised or lowered to suit the tide. So, they rolled the luggage-vans onto the boat and off on the other side; and as I was in one of the apartments adjoining a bag- gage-car, they considered it unnecessary to wake me up, and tumbled me over with the luggage. But when my master was asked to leave his seat, he found it very dark and cold and raining. He missed me for the first time on the journey. On all previous occasions, as soon as the train stopped, I was at hand to assist him. This caused many slaveholders to praise me very much: they said they had never before seen a slave so attentive to his master and therefore my absence filled him with terror and confusion; the children of Israel could not have felt more troubled on arriving at the Red Sea. So, he asked the conductor if he had seen anything of his slave. The man being somewhat of an abolitionist, and believing that my master was really a slaveholder, thought he would tease him a little respecting me. So, he said, "No, sir; I haven't seen anything of him for some time: I have no doubt he has run away and is in Philadelphia, free, long before now." My master knew that there was nothing in this so he asked the conductor if he would be pleased to see if he could find me. The man indignantly replied, "I am no slave-hunter and as far as I am concerned everybody must look after their own niggers." He went off and left the confused invalid to fancy whatever he felt inclined. My master at first thought I must have been kidnapped into slavery by someone, or left, or perhaps killed on the train. He also thought of stopping to see if he could hear anything of me, but he soon remembered that he had no money. That night all the money we had was consigned to my own pocket because we thought, in case there were any pickpockets about, a slave's pocket would be the last one they would look for. However, hoping to meet me some day in a land of liberty and as he had the tickets, he thought it best upon the whole to enter the boat and come off to Philadelphia, and endeavour to make his way alone in this cold and hollow world as best he could. The time was now up, so he went on board and came across with feelings that can be better imagined than described.

After the train had gotten fairly on the way to Philadelphia, the guard came into my car and gave me a violent shake and bawled out at the same time, "Boy, wake up!" I started, almost frightened out of my wits. He said, "Your master is scared half to death about you." That frightened me still more, I thought they had found him out, so I anxiously inquired what was the matter. The guard said, "He thinks you have run away from him." This made me feel quite at ease. I said, "No, sir; I am satisfied my good master doesn't think that." So off I started to see him. He had been fearfully nervous, but on seeing me he at once felt much better. He merely wished to know what had become of me.

On returning to my seat, I found the conductor and two or three other people amusing themselves very much respecting my running away. So, the guard said, "Boy, what did your master want?"* I replied, "He merely wished to know what had become of me." "No," said the man, "that was not it; he thought you had taken French leave, for parts unknown. I never saw a fellow so badly scared about losing his slave in my life. Now," continued the guard, "let me give you a little friendly advice. When you get to Philadelphia, run away and leave that cripple, and have your liberty." "No, sir," I indifferently replied, "I can't promise to do that." "Why not?" said the

*** I may state here that every man slave is called boy till he is very old, then the more respectable slaveholders call him uncle. The women are all girls till they are aged, then they are called aunts. This is the reason why Mrs. Stowe calls her characters Uncle Tom, Aunt Chloe, Uncle Tiff, &c. conductor, evidently much surprised; "don't you want your liberty?" "Yes, sir," I replied, "but I shall never run away from such a good master as I have at present."**

One of the men said to the guard, "Let him alone; I guess he will open his eyes when he gets to Philadelphia and see things in another light." After giving me a good deal of information, which I afterwards found to be very useful, they left me alone.

I also met with a coloured gentleman on this train, who recommended me to a boarding-house that was kept by an abolitionist, where he thought I would be quite safe, if I wished to run away from my master. I thanked him kindly, but of course did not let him know who we were. Late at night, or rather early in the morning, I heard a fearful whistling of the steam-engine, so I opened the window and looked out, and saw a large number of flickering lights in the distance, and heard a passenger in the next carriage, who also had his head out of the window say to his companion, "Wake up, old horse, we are at Philadelphia!"

The sight of those lights and that announcement made me feel almost as happy as Bunyan's Christian must have felt when he first caught sight of the cross. I, like him, felt that the straps that bound the heavy burden to my back began to pop and the load rolled off. I also looked, and looked again, for it appeared very wonderful to me how the mere sight of our first city of refuge should have all at once made my hitherto sad and heavy heart become so light and happy. As the train speeded on, I rejoiced and thanked God with all my heart and soul for his great kindness and tender mercy, in watching over us, and bringing us safely through.

As soon as the train had reached the platform, before it had fairly stopped, I hurried out of my carriage to my master, whom I got at once into a cab, placed the luggage on, jumped in myself, and we drove off to the boarding-house which was so kindly recommended to me. On leaving the station, my master or rather my wife, as I may now say who had from the commencement of the journey borne up in a manner that much surprised us both, grasped me by the hand, and said, "Thank God, William, we are safe!" and then burst into tears, leant upon me, and wept like a child. The reaction was fearful. So, when we reached the house, she was in reality so weak and faint that she could scarcely stand alone. However, I got her into the apartments that were pointed out, and there we knelt down, on this Sabbath, and Christmas-day, a day that will ever be memorable to us and poured out our heartfelt gratitude to God, for his good-ness in enabling us to overcome so many perilous difficulties, in escaping out of the jaws of the wicked.

PART II.

After my wife had a little recovered herself, she threw off the disguise and assumed her own apparel. We then stepped into the sitting-room and asked to see the landlord. The man came in, but he seemed thunderstruck on finding a fugitive slave and his wife, instead of a "young cotton planter and his nigger." As his eyes travelled round the room, he said to me, "Where is your master?" I pointed him out. The man gravely replied, "I am not joking, I really wish to see your master." I pointed him out again, but at first, he could not believe his eyes; he said; "he knew that was not the gentleman that came with me."

But, after some conversation, we satisfied him that we were fugitive slaves, and had just escaped in the manner I have described. We asked him if he thought it would be safe for us to stop in Philadelphia. He said he thought not, but he would call in some people who knew more about the laws than himself. He then went out and kindly brought in several of the leading abolitionists of the city, who gave us a most hearty and friendly welcome amongst them. As it was in December, and also as we had just left a very warm climate, they advised us not to go to Canada as we had intended, but to settle at Boston in the United States. It is true that the constitution of the Re- public has always guaranteed the slaveholders the right to come into any of the so-called free States and take their fugitives back to southern Egypt. But through the untiring, uncompromising, and manly efforts of Mr. Garrison, Wendell Phillips, Theodore Parker, and a host of other noble abolitionists of Boston and the neighbourhood, public opinion in Massachusetts had become so much opposed to slavery and to kidnapping, that it was almost impossible for anyone to take a fugitive slave out of that State.

So, we took the advice of our good Philadelphia friends, and settled at Boston. I shall have some- thing to say about our sojourn there presently.

Among other friends we met with at Philadelphia, was Robert Purves, Esq., a well-educated and wealthy coloured gentleman, who introduced us to Mr. Barkley Ivens, a member of the Society of Friends, and a noble and generous-hearted farmer, who lived at some distance in the country.

This good Samaritan at once invited us to go and stop quietly with his family, till my wife could somewhat recover from the fearful reaction of the past journey. We most gratefully accepted the invitation, and at the time appointed we took a steamer to a place up the Delaware river, where our new and dear friend met us with his snug little cart and took us to his happy home. This was the first act of great and disinterested kindness we had ever received from a white person.

The gentleman was not of the fairest complexion, and therefore, as my wife was not in the room when I received the information respecting him and his anti-slavery character, she thought of course he was a quadroon like herself. But on arriving at the house, and finding out her mistake, she became more nervous and timid than ever.

As the cart came into the yard, the dear good old lady, and her three charming and affectionate daughters, all came to the door to meet us. We got out, and the gentleman said, "Go in, and make yourselves at home; I will see after the baggage." But my wife was afraid to approach them. She stopped in the yard, and said to me, "William, I thought we were coming among coloured people?" I replied, "It is all right; these are the same." "No," she said, "it is not all right, and I am not going to stop here; I have no confidence whatever in white people, they are only trying to get us back to slavery." She turned round and said, "I am going right off." The old lady then came out, with her sweet, soft, and winning smile, shook her heartily by the hand, and kindly said, "How art thou, my dear? We are all very glad to see thee and thy husband. Come in, to the fire; I dare say thou art cold and hungry after thy journey."

We went in, and the young ladies asked if she would like to go upstairs and "fix" herself before tea. My wife said, "No, I thank you; I shall only stop a little while." "But where art thou going this cold night?" said Mr. Ivens, who had just stepped in. "I don't know," was the reply. "Well, then," he continued, "I think thou hadst better take off thy things and sit near the fire; tea will soon be ready. "Yes, come, Ellen," said Mrs. Ivens, "let me assist thee;" (as she commenced undoing my wife's bonnetstrings) "don't be frightened, Ellen, I shall not hurt a single hair of thy head. We have heard with much pleasure of the marvellous escape of thee and thy husband, and deeply sympathize with thee in all that thou hast undergone. I don't wonder at thee, poor thing, being timid but thou needs not fear us; we would as soon send one of our own daughters into slavery as thee so thou mayest make thyself quite at ease!" These soft and soothing words fell like balm upon my wife's unstrung nerves and melted her to tears; her fears and prejudices vanished and from that day she has firmly believed that there are good and bad people of every shade of complexion.

After seeing Sally Ann and Jacob, two coloured domestics, my wife felt quite at home. After partaking of what Mrs. Stowe's Mose and Pete called a "busting supper," the ladies wished to know whether we could read. On learning we could not, they said if we liked they would teach us. To this kind offer, of course, there was no objection. But we looked rather knowingly at each other, as much as to say that they would have rather a hard task to cram anything into our thick and mature skulls.

However, all hands set to and quickly cleared away the tea-things, and the ladies and their good brother brought out the spelling and copy books and slates, &c., and commenced with their new and green pupils. We had, by stratagem, learned the alphabet while in slavery, but not the writing characters and as we had been such a time learning so little, we at first felt that it was a waste of time for anyone at our age to undertake to learn to read and write. But, as the ladies were so anxious that we should learn, and so willing to teach us, we decided to give our whole minds to the work and see what could be done. By so doing, at the end of the three weeks we remained with the good family we could spell and write our names quite legibly. They all begged us to stop longer but as we were not safe in the State of Pennsylvania and also as we wished to commence doing something for a livelihood, we did not remain.

When the time arrived for us to leave for Boston, it was like parting with our relatives. We have since met with many very kind and hospitable friends, both in America and England; but we have never been under a roof where we were made to feel more at home, or where the inmates took a deeper interest in our well-being, than Mr. Barkley Ivens and his dear family. May God ever bless them and preserve each one from every reverse of fortune!

We finally, as I have stated, settled at Boston, where we remained nearly two years, I employed as cabinet-maker and furniture broker and my wife at her needle and as our little earnings in slavery were not all spent on the journey, we were getting on very well, and would have made money, if we had not been compelled by the General Government, at the bidding of the slaveholders to break up business and fly from under the Stars and Stripes to save our liberties and our lives.

In 1850, Congress passed the Fugitive Slave Bill, an enactment too infamous to have been thought of or tolerated by any people in the world, except the unprincipled and tyrannical Yankees. The following are a few of the leading features of the above law, which requires, under heavy penalties, that the inhabitants of the free States should not only refuse food and shelter to a starving, hunted human being, but also should assist, if called upon by the authorities, to seize the unhappy fugitive and send him back to slavery.

In no case is a person's evidence admitted in Court, in defence of his liberty, when arrested under this law.

If the judge decides that the prisoner is a slave, he gets ten dollars but if he sets him at liberty, he only receives five.

After the prisoner has been sentenced to slavery, he is handed over to the United States Marshal, who has the power, at the expense of the General Government, to summon a sufficient force to take the poor creature back to slavery, and to the lash, from which he fled.

Our old masters sent agents to Boston after us. They took out warrants and placed them in the hands of the United States Marshal to execute. But the following letter from our highly esteemed and faithful friend, the Rev. Samuel May of Boston, to our equally dear and much-lamented friend, Dr. Estlin of Bristol, will show why we were not taken into custody.

"21, Cornhill, Boston, "November 6th, 1850.

"My dear Mr Estlin,

"I trust that in God's good providence this letter will be handed to you in safety by our good friends, William and Ellen Craft. They have lived amongst us about two years, and have proved themselves worthy, in all respects, of our confidence and regard. The laws of this republican and Christian land (tell it not in Moscow, nor in Constantinople) regard them only as slave's chattels personal property. But they nobly vindicated their title and right to freedom, two years since, by winning their way to it; at least, so they thought. But now, the slave power, with the aid of Daniel Webster and a band of lesser traitors, has enacted a law, which puts their dearly-bought liberties in the most imminent peril; holds out a strong temptation to every mercenary and unprincipled ruffian to become their kidnapper; and has stimulated the slaveholders generally to such desperate acts for the recovery of their fugitive property, as have never before been enacted in the history of this government.

"Within a fortnight, two fellows from Macon, Georgia, have been in Boston for the purpose of arresting our friends William and Ellen. A writ was served against them from the United States District Court, but it was not served by the United States Marshal; why not, is not certainly known: perhaps through fear, for a general feeling of indignation and a cool determination not to allow this young couple to be taken from Boston into slavery, was aroused, and pervaded the city. It is understood that one of the judges told the Marshal that he would not be authorized in breaking the door of Craft's house. Craft kept himself close within the house, armed himself and awaited with remarkable composure the event. Ellen, in the meantime, had been taken to a retired place out of the city. The Vigilance Committee (appointed at a late meeting in Fanueil Hall) enlarged their numbers, held an almost permanent session, and appointed various sub- committees to act in different ways. One of these committees called repeatedly on Messrs. Hughes and Knight, the slavecatchers, and requested and advised them to leave the city. At first, they peremptorily refused to do so, "till they got hold of the niggers.' On complaint of different persons, these two fellows were several times arrested, carried before one of our county courts, and held to bail on charges of 'conspiracy to kidnap,' and of 'defamation,' in calling William and Ellen 'Slaves.' At length, they became so alarmed that they left the city by an indirect route, evading the vigilance of many people who were on the look-out for them. Hughes, at one time, was near losing his life at the hands of an infuriated coloured man. While these men remained in the city, a prominent Whig gentleman sent word to William Craft, that if he would submit peaceably to an arrest, he and his wife should be bought from their owners, cost what it might. Craft replied, in effect, that he was in a measure the representative of all the other fugitives in Boston, some 200 or 300 in number; that, if he gave up, they would all be at the mercy of the slave-catchers, and must fly from the city at any sacrifice; and that, if his freedom could be bought for two cents, he would not consent to com- promise the matter in such a way. This event has stirred up the slave spirit of the country, south and north; the United States government is determined to try its hand in enforcing the Fugitive Slave law; and William and Ellen Craft would be prominent objects of the slaveholders' vengeance. Under these circumstances, it is the almost unanimous opinion of their best friends, that they should quit America as speedily as possible, and seek asylum in England! Oh! shame, shame upon us, that Americans, whose fathers fought against Great Britain, in order to be Free, should have to acknowledge this disgraceful fact! God gave us a fair and goodly heritage in this land, but man has cursed it with his devices and crimes against human souls and human rights. Is America the 'land of the free, and the home of the brave?' God knows it is not; and we know it too. A brave young man and a virtuous young woman must fly the American shores, and seek, under the shadow of the British throne, the enjoyment of 'life, liberty and the pursuit of happiness.'

"But I must pursue my plain, sad story. All day long, I have been busy planning a safe way for William and Ellen to leave Boston. We dare not allow them to go on board a vessel, even in the port of Boston; for the writ is yet in the Marshal's hands, and he May be waiting an opportunity to serve it so I am expecting to accompany them tomorrow to Portland, Maine, which is beyond the reach of the Marshal's authority and there I hope to see them on board a British steamer.

"This letter is written to introduce them to you. I know your infirm health, but I am sure, if you were stretched on your bed in your last illness and could lift your hand at all, you would extend it to welcome these poor hunted fellow creatures. Hence-forth, England is their nation and their home. It is with real regret for our personal loss in their departure, as well as burning shame for the land that is not worthy of them, that we send them away or rather allow them to go. But, with all the resolute courage they have shown in a most trying hour, they themselves see it is part of a foolhardy rashness to attempt to stay here longer.

"I must close and with many renewed thanks for all your kind words and deeds towards us,

"I am, very respectfully yours,

"SAMUEL MAY, JUN."

Our old masters, having heard how their agents were treated at Boston, wrote to Mr. Filmore, who was then President of the States, to know what he could do to have us sent back to slavery. Mr. Filmore said that we should be returned. He gave instructions for military force to be sent to Boston to assist the officers in making the arrest. Therefore we, as well as our friends (among whom was George Thompson, Esq., late M.P. for the Tower Hamlets, the slave's long-tried, self-sacrificing friend and eloquent advocate) thought it best, at any sacrifice, to leave the mock-free Republic, and come to a country where we and our dear little ones can be truly free. "No one daring to molest or make us afraid." But, as the officers were watching every vessel that left the port to prevent us from escaping, we had to take the expensive and tedious overland route to Halifax.

We shall always cherish the deepest feelings of gratitude to the Vigilance Committee of Boston (upon which were many of the leading abolitionists) and also to our numerous friends, for the very kind and noble manner in which they assisted us to preserve our liberties and to escape from Boston, as it were like Lot from Sodom, to a place of refuge, and finally to this truly free and glorious country; where no tyrant, let his power be ever so absolute over his poor trembling victims at home, dare come and lay violent hands upon us or upon our dear little boys (who had the good fortune to be born upon British soil), and reduce us to the legal level of the beast that perisheth. Oh! May God bless the thousands of unflinching, dis-interested abolitionists of America, who are labouring through evil as well as through good report, to cleanse their country's escutcheon from the foul and destructive blot of slavery, and to restore to every bondman his God-given rights; and may God ever smile upon England and upon England's good, much-beloved, and deservedly-honoured

Queen, for the generous protection that is given to unfortunate refugees of every rank, and of every colour, and clime.

On the passing of the Fugitive Slave Bill, the following learned doctors, as well as a host of lesser traitors, came out strongly in its defence.

The Rev. Dr. Gardiner Spring, an eminent Presbyterian Clergyman of New York, well known in this country by his religious publications, declared from the pulpit that, "if by one prayer he could liberate every slave in the world he would not dare to offer it."

The Rev. Dr. Joel Parker, of Philadelphia, in the course of a discussion on the nature of Slavery, says, "What, then, are the evils inseparable from slavery? There is not one that is not equally inseparable from depraved human nature in other lawful relations."

The Rev. Moses Stuart, D.D., (late Professor in the Theological College of Andover), in his vindication of this Bill, reminds his readers that "many Southern slaveholders are true Christians." That "sending back a fugitive to them is not like restoring one to an idolatrous people." That "though we may PITY the fugitive, yet the Mosaic Law does not authorize the rejection of the claims of the slaveholders to their stolen or strayed Property."

The Rev. Dr. Spencer, of Brooklyn, New York, has come forward in support of the "Fugitive Slave Bill," by publishing a sermon entitled the "Religious Duty of Obedience to the Laws," which has elicited the highest encomiums from Dr. Samuel H. Cox, the Presbyterian minister of Brooklyn (notorious both in this country and America for his sympathy with the slaveholder).

The Rev. W. M. Rogers, an orthodox minister of Boston, delivered a sermon in which he says, "When the slave asks me to stand be- tween him and his master, what does he ask? He asks me to murder a nation's life; and I will not do it, because I have a conscience, because there is a God." He proceeds to affirm that if resistance to the carrying out of the "Fugitive Slave Law" should lead the magistracy to call the citizens to arms, their duty was to obey and "if ordered to take human life, in the name of God to take it;" and he concludes by admonishing the fugitives to "hearken to the Word of God, and to count their own masters worthy of all honour."

The Rev. William Crowell, of Waterfield, State of Maine, printed a Thanksgiving Sermon of the same kind, in which he calls upon his hearers not to allow "excessive sympathies for a few hundred fugitives to blind them so that they may risk increased suffering to the millions already in chains."

The Rev. Dr. Taylor, an Episcopal Clergyman of New Haven, Connecticut, made a speech at a Union Meeting, in which he deprecates the agitation on the law, and urges obedience to it; asking, "Is that article in the Constitution contrary to the law of Nature, of nations, or to the will of God? Is it so? Is there a shadow of reason for saying it? I have not been able to discover it. Have I not shown you it is lawful to deliver up, in compliance with the laws, fugitive slaves, for the high, the great, the momentous interests of those [Southern] States?"

The Right Rev. Bishop Hopkins, of Vermont, in a Lecture at Lockport, says, "It was warranted by the Old Testament;" and inquires, "What effect had the Gospel in doing away with slavery? None whatever." Therefore, he argues, as it is expressly permitted by the Bible, it does not in itself involve any sin; but that every Christian is authorized by the Divine Law to own slaves, provided they were not treated with unnecessary cruelty.

The Rev. Orville Dewey, D.D., of the Unitarian connection, maintained in his lectures that the safety of the Union is not to be hazarded for the sake of the African race. He declares that, for his part, he would send his own brother or child into slavery, if needed to preserve the Union between the free and the slaveholding States; and, counselling the slave to similar magnanimity, thus exhorts him: "YOUR RIGHT TO BE FREE IS NOT ABSOLUTE, UNQUALIFIED, IRRESPECTIVE OF ALL CONSEQUENCES. If my espousal of your claim is likely to involve your race and mine together in disasters infinitely greater than your personal servitude, then you ought not to be free. In such a case personal rights ought to be sacrificed to the general good. You yourself ought to see this and be willing to suffer for a while one for many."

If the Doctor is prepared, he is quite at liberty to sacrifice his "personal rights to the general good." But, as I have suffered a long time in slavery, it is hardly fair for the Doctor to advise me to go back. According to his showing, he ought rather to take my place. That would be practically carrying out his logic, as respects "suffering awhile, one for many."

In fact, so eager were they to prostrate them- selves before the great idol of slavery, and, like Balaam, to curse instead of blessing the people whom God had brought out of bondage, that they in bring up obsolete passages from the Old Testament to justify their downward course, overlooked, or would not see, the following verses, which show very clearly, according to the Doctor's own textbook, that the slaves have a right to run away, and that it is unscriptural for anyone to send them back.

In the 23rd chapter of Deuteronomy, 15th, and 16th verses, it is thus written: "Thou shalt not deliver unto his master the servant which is escaped from his master unto thee. He shall dwell with thee, even among you, in that place which he shall choose in one of thy gates, where it liketh him best: thou shalt not oppress him."

"Hide the outcast. Bewray not him that wandereth. Let my outcasts dwell with thee. Be thou a covert to them from the face of the spoiler." —(Isa. xvi. 3, 4.)

The great majority of the American ministers are not content with uttering sentences similar to the above or remaining wholly indifferent to the cries of the poor bondman; but they do all they can to blast the reputation, and to muzzle the mouths, of the few good men who dare to beseech the God of mercy" to loose the bonds of wickedness, to undo the heavy burdens and let the oppressed go free." These reverend gentlemen pour a terrible cannonade upon "Jonah," for refusing to carry God's message against Nineveh, and tell us about the whale in which he was entombed; while they utterly overlook the existence of the whales which trouble their republican waters and know not that they themselves are the "Jonahs" who threaten to sink their ship of state, by steering in an unrighteous direction. We are told that the whale vomited up the runaway prophet. This would not have seemed so strange had it been one of the above lukewarm Doctor of Divinity whom he had swallowed, for even a whale might find such a morsel difficult of digestion.

"I venerate the man whose heart is warm,
Whose hands are pure; whose doctrines and whose life
Coincident, exhibit lucid proof
That he is honest in the sacred cause."

"But grace abused brings forth the foulest deeds,
As richest soil the most luxuriant weeds."

I must now leave the reverend gentlemen in the hands of Him who knows best how to deal with a recreant ministry.

I do not wish it to be understood that all the ministers of the States are of the Balaam stamp. There are those who are as uncompromising with slaveholders as Moses was with Pharaoh and like Daniel, will never bow down before the great false God that has been set up.

On arriving at Portland, we found that the steamer we intended to take had run into a schooner the previous night and was lying up for repairs so we had to wait there, in fearful suspense, for two or three days. During this time, we had the honour of being the guest of the late and much-lamented Daniel Oliver, Esq., one of the best and most hospitable men in the State. By simply fulfilling the Scripture injunction, to take in the stranger, &c., he ran the risk of incurring a penalty of 2,000 dollars, and twelve months' imprisonment.

But neither the Fugitive Slave Law, nor any other Satanic enactment, can ever drive the spirit of liberty and humanity out of such noble and generous-hearted men.

May God ever bless his dear widow and eventually unite them in His courts above!

We finally got off to St. John's, New Brunswick, where we had to wait two days for the steamer that conveyed us to Windsor, Nova Scotia.

Ongoing into a hotel at St. John's, we met the butler in the hall, to whom I said, "We wish to stop here to-night." He turned round, scratching his head, evidently much put about. But thinking that my wife was white, he replied, "We have plenty of room for the lady, but I don't know about yourself, we never take in coloured folks." "Oh, don't trouble about me," I said; "if you have room for the lady, that will do; so please have the luggage taken to a bedroom." Which was immediately done, and my wife went upstairs into the apartment.

After taking a little walk in the town, I returned, and asked to see the "lady." On being conducted to the little sitting room, where she then was, I entered without knocking, much to the surprise of the whole house. The "lady" then rang the bell and ordered dinner for two. "Dinner for two, mum!" exclaimed the waiter, as he backed out of the door. "Yes, for two," said my wife. In a little while the stout, red-nosed butler, whom we first met, knocked at the door. I called out, "Come in." On entering, he rolled his whisky eyes at me and then at my wife, and said, in a very solemn tone, "Did you order dinner for two, mum?" "Yes, for two," my wife again replied. This confused the chubby butler more than ever and as the landlord was not in the house, he seemed at a loss what to do.

When dinner was ready, the maid came in and said, "Please, mum, the Missis wishes to know whether you will have dinner up now, or wait till your friend arrives?" "I will have it up at once, if you please." "Thank you, mum," continued the maid, and out she glided.

After a good deal of giggling in the passage, someone said, "You are in for it, butler, after all, so you had better make the best of a bad job." But before dinner was sent up, the landlord returned, and having heard from the steward of the steamer by which we came that we were bound for England, the proprietor's native country, he treated us in the most respectful manner.

At the above house, the boots (whose name I for- get) was a fugitive slave, a very intelligent and active man, about forty-five years of age. Soon after his marriage, while in slavery, his bride was sold away from him, and he could never learn where the poor creature dwelt. So, after remaining single for many years, both before and after his escape, and never expecting to see again, nor even to hear from, his long- lost partner, he finally married a woman at St. John's. But, poor fellow, as he was passing down the street one day, he met a woman; at the first glance they nearly recognized each other; they both turned round and stared, and unconsciously advanced, till she screamed and flew into his arms. Her first words were, "Dear, are you married?" On his answering in the affirmative, she shrank from his embrace, hung her head, and wept. A person who witnessed this meeting told me it was most affecting.

This couple knew nothing of each other's escape or whereabouts. The woman had escaped a few years before to the free States, by secreting herself in the hold of a vessel but as they tried to get her back to bondage, she fled to New Brunswick for that protection which her native country was too mean to afford.

The man at once took his old wife to see his new one, who was also a fugitive slave, and as they all knew the workings of the infamous system of slavery, the could (as no one else can,) sympathize with each other's misfortune.

According to the rules of slavery, the man and his first wife were already divorced, but not morally and therefore it was arranged between the three that he should live only with the lastly married wife and allow the other one so much a week, as long as she requested his assistance.

After staying at St. John's two days, the steamer arrived, which took us to Windsor, where we found a coach bound for Halifax. Prejudice against colour forced me to go to the top in the rain. On arriving within about seven miles of the town, the coach broke down and was upset. I fell upon the big crotchety driver, whose head stuck in the mud and as he "always objected to niggers riding inside with white folks," I was not particularly sorry to see him deeper in the mire than myself. All of us were scratched and bruised more or less. After the passengers had crawled out as best, they could, we all set off and paddled through the deep mud and cold and rain, to Halifax.

On leaving Boston, it was our intention to reach Halifax at least two or three days before the steamer from Boston touched there, en route for Liverpool but having been detained so long at Portland and St. John's, we had the misfortune to arrive at Halifax at dark, just two hours after the steamer had gone consequently, we had to wait there a fortnight for the Cambria.

The coach was patched up, and reached Halifax with the luggage, soon after the passengers arrived. The only respectable hotel that was then in the town had suspended business and was closed so we went to the inn, opposite the market, where the coach stopped: a most miserable, dirty hole it was.

Knowing that we were still under the influence of the low Yankee prejudice, I sent my wife in with the other passengers, to engage a bed for herself and husband. I stopped outside in the rain till the coach came up. If I had gone in and asked for a bed, they would have been quite full. But as they thought my wife was white, she had no difficulty in securing apartments, into which the luggage was afterwards carried. The landlady, observing that I took an interest in the baggage, became some- what uneasy and went into my wife's room, and said to her, "Do you know the dark man downstairs?" "Yes, he is my husband." "Oh! I mean the black man the Nigger?" "I quite understand you; he is my husband." "My God!" exclaimed the woman as she flounced out and banged to the door. Ongoing upstairs, I heard what had taken place: but, as we were there, and did not mean to leave that night, we did not disturb ourselves. On our ordering tea, the landlady sent word back to say that we must take it in the kitchen or in our bedroom, as she had no other room for "niggers." We replied that we were not particular and that they could sent it up to our room, which they did.

After the pro-slavery persons who were staying there heard that we were in, the whole house became agitated, and all sorts of oaths and fearful threats were heaped upon the "d——d niggers, for coming among white folks." Some of them said they would not stop there a minute if there was another house to go to.

The mistress came up the next morning to know how long we wished to stop. We stayed a fortnight. "Oh! dear me, it is impossible for us to accommodate you and I think you had better go you must understand, I have no prejudice myself; I think a good deal of the coloured people and have always been their friend but if you stop here, we shall lose all our customers, which we can't do no-how." We said we were glad to hear that she had "no prejudice," and was such a staunch friend to the coloured people. We also informed her that we would be sorry for her "customers" to leave on our account and as it was not our intention to interfere with anyone, it was foolish for them to be frightened away. However, if she would get us a comfortable place, we would be glad to leave. The landlady said she would go out and try. After spending the whole morning in canvassing the town, she came to our room and said, "I have been from one end of the place to the other, but everybody is full." Having a little foretaste of the vulgar prejudice of the town, we did not wonder at this result. However, the landlady gave me the address of some respectable coloured families, whom she thought, "under the circumstances," might be induced to take us. And, as we were not at all comfortable being compelled to sit, eat, and sleep, in the same small room, we were quite willing to change our quarters.

I called upon the Rev. Mr. Cannady, a truly good- hearted Christian man, who received us at a word; and both he and his kind lady treated us handsomely and for a nominal charge.

My wife and myself were both unwell when we left Boston and having caught a fresh cold on the journey to Halifax, we were laid up there under the doctor's care, nearly the whole fortnight. I had much worry about getting tickets, for they baffled us shamefully at the Cunard office. They at first said that they did not book till the steamer came which was not the fact. When I called again, they said they knew the steamer would come full of Boston and therefore we had "better try to get to Liverpool by other means." Other mean Yankee excuses were made; and it was not till an influential gentleman, to whom Mr. Francis Jackson, of Boston, kindly gave us a letter, went, and rebuked them, that we were able to secure our tickets. So, when we went on board my wife was very poorly, and was also so Ill on the voyage that I did not believe she could live to see Liverpool.

However, I am thankful to say she arrived and after laying up at Liverpool very ill for two or three weeks, gradually recovered.

It was not until we stepped upon the shore at Liverpool that we were free from every slavish fear.

We raised our thankful hearts to Heaven, and could have knelt down, like the Neapolitan exiles, and kissed the soil; for we felt that from slavery.

"Heaven sure had kept this spot of earth uncursed,
To show how all things were created first."

In a few days after we landed, the Rev. Francis Bishop and his lady came and invited us to be their guests; to whose unlimited kindness and watchful care my wife owes, in a great degree, her restoration to health.

We enclosed our letter from the Rev. Mr. May to Mr. Estlin, who at once wrote to invite us to his house at Bristol. On arriving there, both Mr. and Miss Estlin received us as cordially as did our first good Quaker friends in Pennsylvania. It grieves me much to have to mention that he is no more. Everyone who knew him can truthfully say.

"Peace to the memory of a man of worth,
A man of letters, and of manners too!
Of manners sweet as Virtue always wears
When gay Good-nature dresses her in smiles."

It was principally through the extreme kindness of Mr. Estlin, the Right Hon. Lady Noel Byron, Miss Harriet Martineau, Mrs. Reid, Miss Sturch, and a few other good friends, that my wife and I were able to spend a short time at a school in this country, to acquire a little of that education which we were so shamefully deprived of while in the house of bondage. The school is under the super- vision of the Misses Lushington, D.C.L. During our stay at the school, we received the greatest attention from everyone, and I am particularly indebted to Thomas Wilson, Esq., of Bradmore House, Chis-wick, (who was then the master,) for the deep interest he took in trying to get me on in my studies. We shall ever fondly and gratefully cherish the memory of our endeared and departed friend, Mr. Estlin. We, as well as the Anti-Slavery cause, lost a good friend in him. However, if departed spirits in Heaven are conscious of the wickedness of this world, and are allowed to speak, he will never fail to plead in the presence of the angelic host, and before the great and just Judge, for down- trodden and outraged humanity.

"Therefore, I cannot think thee wholly gone;
The better part of thee is with us still;
Thy soul its hampering clay aside hath thrown,
And only freer wrestles with the ill.

"Thou livest in the life of all good things;
What words thou spak'st for Freedom shall not die;
Thou sleepest not, for now thy Love hath wings
To soar where hence thy hope could hardly fly.

"And often, from that other world, on this
Some gleams from great souls gone before may shine,
To shed on struggling hearts a clearer bliss,
And clothe the Right with lustre more divine.

"Farewell! good man, good angel now! this hand
Soon, like thine own, shall lose its cunning, too;
Soon shall this soul, like thine, bewildered stand,
Then leap to thread the free unfathomed blue."

JAMES RUSSELL LOWELL.

In the preceding pages I have not dwelt upon the great barbarities which are practiced upon the slaves; because I wish to present the system in its mildest form, and to show that the "tender mercies of the wicked are cruel." But I do now, however, most solemnly declare, that a very large majority of the American slaves are over-worked, under-fed, and frequently unmercifully flogged.

I have often seen slaves tortured in every conceivable manner. I have seen him hunted down and torn by bloodhounds. I have seen them shamefully beaten and branded with hot irons. I have seen them hunted, and even burned alive at the stake, frequently for offences that would be applauded if committed by white persons for similar purposes.

In short, it is well known in England, if not all over the world, that the Americans, as a people are notoriously mean and cruel towards all coloured persons, whether they are bond or free.

"Oh, tyrant, thou who sleepest
On a volcano, from whose pent-up wrath,
Already some red flashes bursting up,
Beware!"

LIST OF TITLES WITH ISBN NO.

ISBN	TITLE
9788194914129	1984
9789390575220	1984 & Animal Farm (2In1)
9789390575572	1984 & Animal Farm (2In1): The International Best-Selling Classics
9789390575848	35 Sonnets
9789390575329	A Clergyman's Daughter
9789390575923	A Study In Scarlet
9789390896097	A Tale Of Two Cities
9789390896837	Abide in Christ
9789390896202	Abraham Lincoln
9789390896912	Absolute Surrender
9789390896608	African American Classic Collection
9789390575305	Aldous Huxley: The Collected Works
9789390896141	An Autobiography of M. K. Gandhi
9789390575886	Animal Farm
9789390575619	Animal Farm & The Great Gatsby (2In1)
9789390575626	Animal Farm & We
9789390896158	Anna Karenina
9789390575534	Antic Hay
9789390896165	Antony & Cleopatra
9789390896172	As I Lay Dying
9789390896226	As You like it
9789390575671	At Your Command
9789390575350	Awakened Imagination
9789390575114	Be What You Wish
9789390896233	Believe In yourself
9789390896998	Best of Charles Darwin: The Origin of Species & Autobiography
9789390896684	Best Of Horror : Dracula And Frankenstein
9789390575503	Best Of Mark Twain (The Adventures of Tom Sawyer AND The Adventures of Huckleberry Finn)
9789390896769	Black History Collection
9789390575756	Brave New World, Animal Farm & 1984 (3in1)

9789390896240	Brother Karamzov
9789390575053	Bulleh Shah Poetry
9789390575725	Burmese Days
9789390896257	Bushido
9789390896066	Can't Hurt Me
9788194914112	Chanakya Neeti: With The Complete Sutras
9789390896042	Crime and Punishment
9789390575527	Crome Yellow
9789390575046	Down and Out in Paris and London
9789390896844	Dracula
9789390575442	Emersons Essays: The Complete First & Second Series (Self-Reliance & Other Essays)
9789390575749	Emma
9789390575817	Essential Tozer Collection - The Pursuit of God & The Purpose of Man
9789390896578	Fascism What It Is and How to Fight It
9789390575688	Feeling is the Secret
9789390575190	Five Lessons
9789390575954	Frankenstein
9789390575237	Franz Kafka: Collected Works
9789390575282	Franz Kafka: Short Stories
9789390575060	George Orwell Collected Works
9789390575077	George Orwell Essays
9789390575213	George Orwell Poems
9788194914150	Greatest Poetry Ever Written Vol 1
9788194914143	Greatest Poetry Ever Written Vol 1
9789390896301	Gulliver's Travel
9789390575961	Gunaho Ka Devta
9789390575893	H. P. Lovecraft Selected Stories Vol 1
9789390575978	H. P. Lovecraft Selected Stories Vol 2
9789390896059	Hamlet
9789390575022	His Last Bow: Some Reminiscences of Sherlock Holmes
9789390896134	History of Western Philosophy
9789390575121	Homage To Catalonia

9789390896219	How to develop self-confidence and Improve public Speaking
9789390896295	How to enjoy your life and your Job
9789390575633	How to own your own mind
9789390896318	How to read Human Nature
9789390896325	How to sell your way through the life
9789390896370	How to use the laws of mind
9789390896387	How to use the power of prayer
9789390896028	How to win friends & Influence People
9788194824176	How To Win Friends and Influence People
9789390896103	Humility The Beauty of Holiness
9789390896653	Imperialism the Highest Stage of Capitalism
9789390575084	In Our Time
9789390575169	In Our Time & Three Stories and Ten poems
9789390575145	James Allen: The Collected Works
9789390896189	Jesus Himself
9789390575480	Jo's Boys
9789390896394	Julius Caesar
9789390575404	Keep the Aspidistra Flying
9789390896400	Kidnapped
9789390896424	King Lear
9789390575824	Lady Susan
9789390896455	Law of Success
9789390896264	Lincoln The Unknown
9789390575565	Little Men
9789390575640	Little Women
9788194914174	Lost Horizon
9789390896462	Macbeth
9789390896929	Man Eaters of Kumaon
9789390896523	Man The Dwelling Place of God
9789390896349	Man The Dwelling Place of God
9789390575909	Mansfield Park
9788194914136	Manto Ki 25 Sarvshreshth Kahaniya
9789390896509	Marxism, Anarchism, Communism
9789390575664	Mathematical Principles of Natural Philosophy

9788194914198	Meditations
9789390575800	Mein Kampf
9789390575794	Memory How To Develop, Train, And Use It
9789390896486	Mind Power
9789390896585	Money
9789390575039	Mortal Coils
9789390575770	My Life and Work
9789390896035	Narrative of the Life of Frederick Douglass
9789390575152	Neville Goddard: The Collected Works
9789390575985	Northanger Abbey
9789390896530	Notes From Underground
9789390896547	Oliver Twist
9789390575459	On War
9789390575541	One, None and a Hundred Thousand
9789390896554	Othelo
9789390575435	Out Of This World
9789390575015	Persuasion
9789390575510	Prayer The Art Of Believing
9789390575091	Pride and Prejudice
9789390896561	Psychic Perception
9789390575381	Rabindranath Tagore - 5 Best Short Stories Vol 2
9789390575367	Rabindranath Tagore - Short Stories (Masters Collections Including The Childs Return)
9789390575374	Rabindranath Tagore 5 Best Short Stories Vol 1 (Including The Childs Return
9789390896622	Romeo & Juliet
9789390896127	Sanatana Dharma
9789390575596	Seedtime & Harvest
9789390896639	Selected Stories of Guy De Maupassant
9789390575206	Self-Reliance & Other Essays
9789390575176	Sense and Sensibility
9789390575299	Shyamchi Aai
9789390896738	Socialism Utopian and Scientific
9789390896646	Success Through a Positive Mental Attitude
9789390575428	The Adventures of Huckleberry Finn

9789390575183	The Adventures of Sherlock Holmes
9789390575343	The Adventures of Tom Sawyer
9789390896691	The Alchemy Of Happiness
9789390575862	The Art Of Public Speaking
9789390896288	The Autobiography Of Charles Darwin
9788194914181	The Best of Franz Kafka: The Metamorphosis & The Trial
9789390575008	The Call Of Cthulhu and Other Weird Tales
9789390575107	The Case-Book of Sherlock Holmes
9789390896110	The Castle Of Otranto
9789390896745	The Communist Manifesto
9789390575589	The Complete Fiction of H. P. Lovecraft
9789390575497	The Complete Works of Florence Scovel Shinn
9789390896820	The Conquest of Breard
9789390896813	The Diary of a Young Girl
9789390896332	The Diary of a Young Girl The Definitive Edition of the Worlds Most Famous Diary
9789390575701	The Great Gatsby, Animal Farm & 1984 (3In1)
9789390575312	The Greatest Works Of George Orwell (5 Books) Including 1984 & Non-Fiction
9789390575992	The Hound of Baskervilles
9789390896707	The Idiot
9789390896714	The Invisible Man
9789390575657	The Knowledge of the holy
9789390575558	The Law & the Promise
9789390896721	The Law Of Attraction
9789390896776	The Leader in you
9789390896363	The Life of Christ
9789390896196	The Man-Eating Leopard of Rudraprayag
9789390896783	The Master Key to Riches
9789390575268	The Memoirs Of Sherlock Holmes
9789390896479	The Midsummer Night's Dream
9789390575466	The Mill On The Floss
9789390896790	The Miracles of your mind
9789390896660	The Mutual Aid A Factor in Evolution
9789390896448	The Origin of Species

9789390896905	The Peter Kropotkin Anthology The Conquest of Bread & Mutual Aid A Factor of Evolution
9789390896806	The Picture of Dorian Gray
9789390896271	The Picture of Dorian Gray
9789390575275	The Power Of Awareness
9789390896356	The Power of Concentration
9788194824169	The Power of Positive Thinking
9789390575411	The Power of the Spoken Word
9788194914105	The Power Of Your Subconscious Mind
9789390896899	The Power of Your Subconscious Mind
9789390896417	The Principles of Communism
9789390575787	The Psychology Of Mans Possible Evolution
9789390896615	The Psychology of Salesmanship
9789390575732	The Pursuit of God
9789390575398	The Pursuit of Happiness
9789390896851	The Quick and Easy Way to effective Speaking
9789390575947	The Return Of Sherlock Holmes
9789390575138	The Road To Wigan Pier
9789390896981	The Root of the Righteous
9789390575855	The Science Of Being Well
9788194914167	The Science Of Getting Rich, The Science Of Being Great & The Science Of Being Well (3In1)
9789390896011	The Screwtape Letters
9789390896073	The Screwtape Letters
9789390575336	The Secret Door to Success
9789390575695	The Secret Of Imagining
9789390896868	The Secret Of Success
9789390896431	The Seven Last Words
9789390575930	The Sign of the Four
9789390896004	The Sonnets
9789390896516	The Souls of Black Folk
9789390896875	The Sound and The Fury
9789390575244	The State and Revolution
9789390896882	The Story of My Life
9789390896936	The Story Of Oriental Philosophy

9789390896752	The Strange Case of Dr. Jekyll and Mr. Hyde
9789390896943	The Tempest
9789390575916	The Valley Of Fear
9789390575879	The Wind in the willows
9789390896080	The Wind in the willows
9789390575763	Their eyes were watching gofd
9789390575831	Three Stories
9789390896950	Twelfth Night
9789390896592	Twelve Years a Slave
9789390896677	Up from Slavery
9789390896974	Value Price and Profit
9789390896967	Wake Up and Live
9789390896493	With Christ in the School of Prayer
9789390575602	Your Faith is Your Fortune
9789390575473	Your Infinite Power To Be Rich
9789390575251	Your Word is Your Wand
9789390575718	Youth
9789391316099	A Christmas Carol
9789391316105	A Doll's House
9789391316501	A Passage to India
9789391316709	A Portrait of the Artist as a Young Man
9789391316112	A Tale of Two Cities
9789391316747	A Tear and a Smile
9789391316167	Agnes Gray
9789391316174	Alice's Adventures in Wonderland
9789391316136	Anandamath
9789391316181	Anne Of Green Gables
9789391316754	Anthem
9789391316198	Around The World in 80 Days
9789391316013	As A Man Thinketh
9789391316242	Autobiography of a Yogi
9789391316266	Beyond Good and Evil
9789391316761	Bleak House
9789391316778	Chitra, a Play in One Act
9789391316310	David Copperfield

9789391316075	Demian
9789391316785	Dubliners
9789391316051	Favourite Tales from the Arabian Nights
9789391316235	Gitanjali
9789391316068	Gravity
9789391316150	Great Speeches of Abraham Lincoln
9789391316662	Guerilla Warfare
9789391316839	Kim
9789391316822	Mother
9789391316211	My Childhood
9789391316846	Nationalism
9789391316327	Oliver Twist
9789391316853	Pygmalion
9789391316334	Relativity: The Special and the General Theory
9789391316389	Scientific Healing Affirmation
9789391316341	Sons and Lovers
9789391316587	Tales from India
9789391316372	Tess of The D'Urbervilles
9789391316396	The Awakening and Selected Stories
9789391316402	The Bhagvad Gita
9789391316303	The Book of Enoch
9789391316228	The Canterville Ghost
9789391316907	The Dynamic Laws of Prosperity
9789391316006	The Great Gatsby
9789391316860	The Hungry Stones and Other Stories
9789391316433	The Idiot
9789391316440	The Importance of Being Earnest
9789391316297	The Light of Asia
9789391316914	The Madman His Parables and Poems
9789391316457	The Odyssey
9789391316921	The Picture of Dorian Gray
9789391316464	The Prince
9789391316938	The Prophet
9789391316945	The Republic
9789391316518	The Scarlet Letter

9789391316143	The Seven Laws of Teaching
9789391316525	The Story of My Experiments with Truth
9789391316532	The Tales of the Mother Goose
9789391316549	The Thirty Nine Steps
9789391316594	The Time Machine
9789391316600	The Turn of the Screw
9789391316983	The Upanishads
9789391316617	The Yellow Wallpaper
9789391316426	The Yoga Sutras of Patanjali
9789391316990	Ulysses
9789391316624	Utopia
9789391316679	Vanity Fair
9789391316020	What Is To Be Done
9789391316686	Within A Budding Grove
9789391316693	Women in Love

www.ingramcontent.com/pod-product-compliance
Lightning Source LLC
LaVergne TN
LVHW101927220826
846093LV00009B/394

* 9 7 8 8 1 1 9 0 0 7 9 2 9 *